C-1596   **CAREER EXAMINATION SERIES**

This is your
PASSBOOK for...

Payroll Clerk

Test Preparation Study Guide
Questions & Answers

COPYRIGHT NOTICE

This book is SOLELY intended for, is sold ONLY to, and its use is RESTRICTED to individual, bona fide applicants or candidates who qualify by virtue of having seriously filed applications for appropriate license, certificate, professional and/or promotional advancement, higher school matriculation, scholarship, or other legitimate requirements of education and/or governmental authorities.

This book is NOT intended for use, class instruction, tutoring, training, duplication, copying, reprinting, excerption, or adaptation, etc., by:

1) Other publishers
2) Proprietors and/or Instructors of "Coaching" and/or Preparatory Courses
3) Personnel and/or Training Divisions of commercial, industrial, and governmental organizations
4) Schools, colleges, or universities and/or their departments and staffs, including teachers and other personnel
5) Testing Agencies or Bureaus
6) Study groups which seek by the purchase of a single volume to copy and/or duplicate and/or adapt this material for use by the group as a whole without having purchased individual volumes for each of the members of the group
7) Et al.

Such persons would be in violation of appropriate Federal and State statutes.

PROVISION OF LICENSING AGREEMENTS – Recognized educational, commercial, industrial, and governmental institutions and organizations, and others legitimately engaged in educational pursuits, including training, testing, and measurement activities, may address request for a licensing agreement to the copyright owners, who will determine whether, and under what conditions, including fees and charges, the materials in this book may be used them. In other words, a licensing facility exists for the legitimate use of the material in this book on other than an individual basis. However, it is asseverated and affirmed here that the material in this book CANNOT be used without the receipt of the express permission of such a licensing agreement from the Publishers. Inquiries re licensing should be addressed to the company, attention rights and permissions department.

All rights reserved, including the right of reproduction in whole or in part, in any form or by any means, electronic or mechanical, including photocopying, recording, or by any information storage and retrieval system, without permission in writing from the Publisher.

Copyright © 2024 by
National Learning Corporation

212 Michael Drive, Syosset, NY 11791
(516) 921-8888 • www.passbooks.com
E-mail: info@passbooks.com

PUBLISHED IN THE UNITED STATES OF AMERICA

PASSBOOK® SERIES

THE *PASSBOOK® SERIES* has been created to prepare applicants and candidates for the ultimate academic battlefield – the examination room.

At some time in our lives, each and every one of us may be required to take an examination – for validation, matriculation, admission, qualification, registration, certification, or licensure.

Based on the assumption that every applicant or candidate has met the basic formal educational standards, has taken the required number of courses, and read the necessary texts, the *PASSBOOK® SERIES* furnishes the one special preparation which may assure passing with confidence, instead of failing with insecurity. Examination questions – together with answers – are furnished as the basic vehicle for study so that the mysteries of the examination and its compounding difficulties may be eliminated or diminished by a sure method.

This book is meant to help you pass your examination provided that you qualify and are serious in your objective.

The entire field is reviewed through the huge store of content information which is succinctly presented through a provocative and challenging approach – the question-and-answer method.

A climate of success is established by furnishing the correct answers at the end of each test.

You soon learn to recognize types of questions, forms of questions, and patterns of questioning. You may even begin to anticipate expected outcomes.

You perceive that many questions are repeated or adapted so that you can gain acute insights, which may enable you to score many sure points.

You learn how to confront new questions, or types of questions, and to attack them confidently and work out the correct answers.

You note objectives and emphases, and recognize pitfalls and dangers, so that you may make positive educational adjustments.

Moreover, you are kept fully informed in relation to new concepts, methods, practices, and directions in the field.

You discover that you are actually taking the examination all the time: you are preparing for the examination by "taking" an examination, not by reading extraneous and/or supererogatory textbooks.

In short, this PASSBOOK®, used directedly, should be an important factor in helping you to pass your test.

PAYROLL CLERK

DUTIES
Under direction of Supervising Payroll Clerk, assists in the performance of clerical duties in the preparation of payrolls and the maintenance of payroll and related records.

This is a very responsible clerical and accounting position which involves the verification and processing of assigned payrolls, personnel reports, and changes relative to the payroll process. Aside from the standard procedures, the involvement in the payroll process requires the incumbent to thoroughly understand the payroll process and the personnel records pertaining to payroll and to constantly be alert for discrepancies. The incumbent receives general supervision from a department administrator. There is little opportunity for independent judgment as the work must be performed in accordance with prescribed policies, procedures, and laws. Does related work as required.

TYPICAL TASKS
Assists in the preparation of the following: Computes the deductions made from salaries for withholding taxes, social security, Federal and State taxes, retirement, medical insurance and wage assignments; when necessary, adjusts payroll checks at conclusion of budget year to coincide with annual salary; computes allowances for vacations, sick leave, and personal leave, and maintains permanent individual records covering same; computes allowances in the longevity program for various classes of government employees; computes and arranges payment on semi-annual basis for employees' night differential; maintains all payroll controls; responsible for routing departmental correspondence; and under supervision, implements new procedures for the functioning of the department.

SCOPE OF THE EXAMINATION
The written test is designed to evaluate knowledge, skills and/or abilities in the following areas:
1. **Arithmetic computation** - These questions test for the ability to use a calculator to do basic computations. Questions will involve addition, subtraction, multiplication and division. You may also be asked to calculate averages, to use percents, and to round an answer to the nearest whole number.
2. **Name and number checking** - These questions test for the ability to distinguish between sets of words, letters, and/or numbers that are almost exactly alike. Material is usually presented in two or three columns, and you will have to determine how the entry in the first column compares with the entry in the second column and possibly the third. You will be instructed to mark your answers according to a designated code provided in the directions.
3. **Office record keeping** - These questions test your ability to perform common office record keeping tasks. The test consists of two or more "sets" of questions, each set concerning a different problem. Typical record keeping problems might involve the organization or collation of data from several sources; scheduling; maintaining a record system using running balances; or completion of a table summarizing data using totals, subtotals, averages and percents.
4. **Operations with Letters and Numbers** - These questions test for skills and abilities in operations involving alphabetizing, comparing, checking and counting. The questions require you to follow the specific directions given for each question which may involve alphabetizing, comparing, checking and counting given groups of letters and/or numbers.
5. **Public contact principles and practices** - These questions test for knowledge of techniques used to interact with other people, to gather and present information, and to provide assistance, advice, and effective customer service in a courteous and professional manner. Questions will cover such topics as understanding and responding to people with diverse needs, perspectives, personalities, and levels of familiarity with agency operations, as well as acting in a way that both serves the public and reflects well on your agency.

HOW TO TAKE A TEST

I. YOU MUST PASS AN EXAMINATION

A. WHAT EVERY CANDIDATE SHOULD KNOW

Examination applicants often ask us for help in preparing for the written test. What can I study in advance? What kinds of questions will be asked? How will the test be given? How will the papers be graded?

As an applicant for a civil service examination, you may be wondering about some of these things. Our purpose here is to suggest effective methods of advance study and to describe civil service examinations.

Your chances for success on this examination can be increased if you know how to prepare. Those "pre-examination jitters" can be reduced if you know what to expect. You can even experience an adventure in good citizenship if you know why civil service exams are given.

B. WHY ARE CIVIL SERVICE EXAMINATIONS GIVEN?

Civil service examinations are important to you in two ways. As a citizen, you want public jobs filled by employees who know how to do their work. As a job seeker, you want a fair chance to compete for that job on an equal footing with other candidates. The best-known means of accomplishing this two-fold goal is the competitive examination.

Exams are widely publicized throughout the nation. They may be administered for jobs in federal, state, city, municipal, town or village governments or agencies.

Any citizen may apply, with some limitations, such as the age or residence of applicants. Your experience and education may be reviewed to see whether you meet the requirements for the particular examination. When these requirements exist, they are reasonable and applied consistently to all applicants. Thus, a competitive examination may cause you some uneasiness now, but it is your privilege and safeguard.

C. HOW ARE CIVIL SERVICE EXAMS DEVELOPED?

Examinations are carefully written by trained technicians who are specialists in the field known as "psychological measurement," in consultation with recognized authorities in the field of work that the test will cover. These experts recommend the subject matter areas or skills to be tested; only those knowledges or skills important to your success on the job are included. The most reliable books and source materials available are used as references. Together, the experts and technicians judge the difficulty level of the questions.

Test technicians know how to phrase questions so that the problem is clearly stated. Their ethics do not permit "trick" or "catch" questions. Questions may have been tried out on sample groups, or subjected to statistical analysis, to determine their usefulness.

Written tests are often used in combination with performance tests, ratings of training and experience, and oral interviews. All of these measures combine to form the best-known means of finding the right person for the right job.

II. HOW TO PASS THE WRITTEN TEST

A. NATURE OF THE EXAMINATION

To prepare intelligently for civil service examinations, you should know how they differ from school examinations you have taken. In school you were assigned certain definite pages to read or subjects to cover. The examination questions were quite detailed and usually emphasized memory. Civil service exams, on the other hand, try to discover your present ability to perform the duties of a position, plus your potentiality to learn these duties. In other words, a civil service exam attempts to predict how successful you will be. Questions cover such a broad area that they cannot be as minute and detailed as school exam questions.

In the public service similar kinds of work, or positions, are grouped together in one "class." This process is known as *position-classification*. All the positions in a class are paid according to the salary range for that class. One class title covers all of these positions, and they are all tested by the same examination.

B. FOUR BASIC STEPS

1) Study the announcement

How, then, can you know what subjects to study? Our best answer is: "Learn as much as possible about the class of positions for which you've applied." The exam will test the knowledge, skills and abilities needed to do the work.

Your most valuable source of information about the position you want is the official exam announcement. This announcement lists the training and experience qualifications. Check these standards and apply only if you come reasonably close to meeting them.

The brief description of the position in the examination announcement offers some clues to the subjects which will be tested. Think about the job itself. Review the duties in your mind. Can you perform them, or are there some in which you are rusty? Fill in the blank spots in your preparation.

Many jurisdictions preview the written test in the exam announcement by including a section called "Knowledge and Abilities Required," "Scope of the Examination," or some similar heading. Here you will find out specifically what fields will be tested.

2) Review your own background

Once you learn in general what the position is all about, and what you need to know to do the work, ask yourself which subjects you already know fairly well and which need improvement. You may wonder whether to concentrate on improving your strong areas or on building some background in your fields of weakness. When the announcement has specified "some knowledge" or "considerable knowledge," or has used adjectives like "beginning principles of..." or "advanced ... methods," you can get a clue as to the number and difficulty of questions to be asked in any given field. More questions, and hence broader coverage, would be included for those subjects which are more important in the work. Now weigh your strengths and weaknesses against the job requirements and prepare accordingly.

3) Determine the level of the position

Another way to tell how intensively you should prepare is to understand the level of the job for which you are applying. Is it the entering level? In other words, is this the position in which beginners in a field of work are hired? Or is it an intermediate or advanced level? Sometimes this is indicated by such words as "Junior" or "Senior" in the class title. Other jurisdictions use Roman numerals to designate the level – Clerk I, Clerk II, for example. The word "Supervisor" sometimes appears in the title. If the level is not indicated by the title, check the description of duties. Will you be working under very close supervision, or will you have responsibility for independent decisions in this work?

4) Choose appropriate study materials

Now that you know the subjects to be examined and the relative amount of each subject to be covered, you can choose suitable study materials. For beginning level jobs, or even advanced ones, if you have a pronounced weakness in some aspect of your training, read a modern, standard textbook in that field. Be sure it is up to date and has general coverage. Such books are normally available at your library, and the librarian will be glad to help you locate one. For entry-level positions, questions of appropriate difficulty are chosen – neither highly advanced questions, nor those too simple. Such questions require careful thought but not advanced training.

If the position for which you are applying is technical or advanced, you will read more advanced, specialized material. If you are already familiar with the basic principles of your field, elementary textbooks would waste your time. Concentrate on advanced textbooks and technical periodicals. Think through the concepts and review difficult problems in your field.

These are all general sources. You can get more ideas on your own initiative, following these leads. For example, training manuals and publications of the government agency which employs workers in your field can be useful, particularly for technical and professional positions. A letter or visit to the government department involved may result in more specific study suggestions, and certainly will provide you with a more definite idea of the exact nature of the position you are seeking.

III. KINDS OF TESTS

Tests are used for purposes other than measuring knowledge and ability to perform specified duties. For some positions, it is equally important to test ability to make adjustments to new situations or to profit from training. In others, basic mental abilities not dependent on information are essential. Questions which test these things may not appear as pertinent to the duties of the position as those which test for knowledge and information. Yet they are often highly important parts of a fair examination. For very general questions, it is almost impossible to help you direct your study efforts. What we can do is to point out some of the more common of these general abilities needed in public service positions and describe some typical questions.

1) General information

Broad, general information has been found useful for predicting job success in some kinds of work. This is tested in a variety of ways, from vocabulary lists to questions about current events. Basic background in some field of work, such as sociology or economics, may be sampled in a group of questions. Often these are principles which have become familiar to most persons through exposure rather than through formal training. It is difficult to advise you how to study for these questions; being alert to the world around you is our best suggestion.

2) Verbal ability

An example of an ability needed in many positions is verbal or language ability. Verbal ability is, in brief, the ability to use and understand words. Vocabulary and grammar tests are typical measures of this ability. Reading comprehension or paragraph interpretation questions are common in many kinds of civil service tests. You are given a paragraph of written material and asked to find its central meaning.

3) Numerical ability

Number skills can be tested by the familiar arithmetic problem, by checking paired lists of numbers to see which are alike and which are different, or by interpreting charts and graphs. In the latter test, a graph may be printed in the test booklet which you are asked to use as the basis for answering questions.

4) Observation

A popular test for law-enforcement positions is the observation test. A picture is shown to you for several minutes, then taken away. Questions about the picture test your ability to observe both details and larger elements.

5) Following directions

In many positions in the public service, the employee must be able to carry out written instructions dependably and accurately. You may be given a chart with several columns, each column listing a variety of information. The questions require you to carry out directions involving the information given in the chart.

6) Skills and aptitudes

Performance tests effectively measure some manual skills and aptitudes. When the skill is one in which you are trained, such as typing or shorthand, you can practice. These tests are often very much like those given in business school or high school courses. For many of the other skills and aptitudes, however, no short-time preparation can be made. Skills and abilities natural to you or that you have developed throughout your lifetime are being tested.

Many of the general questions just described provide all the data needed to answer the questions and ask you to use your reasoning ability to find the answers. Your best preparation for these tests, as well as for tests of facts and ideas, is to be at your physical and mental best. You, no doubt, have your own methods of getting into an exam-taking mood and keeping "in shape." The next section lists some ideas on this subject.

IV. KINDS OF QUESTIONS

Only rarely is the "essay" question, which you answer in narrative form, used in civil service tests. Civil service tests are usually of the short-answer type. Full instructions for answering these questions will be given to you at the examination. But in case this is your first experience with short-answer questions and separate answer sheets, here is what you need to know:

1) Multiple-choice Questions

Most popular of the short-answer questions is the "multiple choice" or "best answer" question. It can be used, for example, to test for factual knowledge, ability to solve problems or judgment in meeting situations found at work.

A multiple-choice question is normally one of three types—

- It can begin with an incomplete statement followed by several possible endings. You are to find the one ending which *best* completes the statement, although some of the others may not be entirely wrong.
- It can also be a complete statement in the form of a question which is answered by choosing one of the statements listed.

- It can be in the form of a problem – again you select the best answer.

Here is an example of a multiple-choice question with a discussion which should give you some clues as to the method for choosing the right answer:

When an employee has a complaint about his assignment, the action which will *best* help him overcome his difficulty is to
- A. discuss his difficulty with his coworkers
- B. take the problem to the head of the organization
- C. take the problem to the person who gave him the assignment
- D. say nothing to anyone about his complaint

In answering this question, you should study each of the choices to find which is best. Consider choice "A" – Certainly an employee may discuss his complaint with fellow employees, but no change or improvement can result, and the complaint remains unresolved. Choice "B" is a poor choice since the head of the organization probably does not know what assignment you have been given, and taking your problem to him is known as "going over the head" of the supervisor. The supervisor, or person who made the assignment, is the person who can clarify it or correct any injustice. Choice "C" is, therefore, correct. To say nothing, as in choice "D," is unwise. Supervisors have and interest in knowing the problems employees are facing, and the employee is seeking a solution to his problem.

2) True/False Questions

The "true/false" or "right/wrong" form of question is sometimes used. Here a complete statement is given. Your job is to decide whether the statement is right or wrong.

SAMPLE: A roaming cell-phone call to a nearby city costs less than a non-roaming call to a distant city.

This statement is wrong, or false, since roaming calls are more expensive.

This is not a complete list of all possible question forms, although most of the others are variations of these common types. You will always get complete directions for answering questions. Be sure you understand *how* to mark your answers – ask questions until you do.

V. RECORDING YOUR ANSWERS

Computer terminals are used more and more today for many different kinds of exams.

For an examination with very few applicants, you may be told to record your answers in the test booklet itself. Separate answer sheets are much more common. If this separate answer sheet is to be scored by machine – and this is often the case – it is highly important that you mark your answers correctly in order to get credit.

An electronic scoring machine is often used in civil service offices because of the speed with which papers can be scored. Machine-scored answer sheets must be marked with a pencil, which will be given to you. This pencil has a high graphite content which responds to the electronic scoring machine. As a matter of fact, stray dots may register as answers, so do not let your pencil rest on the answer sheet while you are pondering the correct answer. Also, if your pencil lead breaks or is otherwise defective, ask for another.

Since the answer sheet will be dropped in a slot in the scoring machine, be careful not to bend the corners or get the paper crumpled.

The answer sheet normally has five vertical columns of numbers, with 30 numbers to a column. These numbers correspond to the question numbers in your test booklet. After each number, going across the page are four or five pairs of dotted lines. These short dotted lines have small letters or numbers above them. The first two pairs may also have a "T" or "F" above the letters. This indicates that the first two pairs only are to be used if the questions are of the true-false type. If the questions are multiple choice, disregard the "T" and "F" and pay attention only to the small letters or numbers.

Answer your questions in the manner of the sample that follows:

32. The largest city in the United States is
    A. Washington, D.C.
    B. New York City
    C. Chicago
    D. Detroit
    E. San Francisco

1) Choose the answer you think is best. (New York City is the largest, so "B" is correct.)
2) Find the row of dotted lines numbered the same as the question you are answering. (Find row number 32)
3) Find the pair of dotted lines corresponding to the answer. (Find the pair of lines under the mark "B.")
4) Make a solid black mark between the dotted lines.

VI. BEFORE THE TEST

Common sense will help you find procedures to follow to get ready for an examination. Too many of us, however, overlook these sensible measures. Indeed, nervousness and fatigue have been found to be the most serious reasons why applicants fail to do their best on civil service tests. Here is a list of reminders:

- Begin your preparation early – Don't wait until the last minute to go scurrying around for books and materials or to find out what the position is all about.
- Prepare continuously – An hour a night for a week is better than an all-night cram session. This has been definitely established. What is more, a night a week for a month will return better dividends than crowding your study into a shorter period of time.
- Locate the place of the exam – You have been sent a notice telling you when and where to report for the examination. If the location is in a different town or otherwise unfamiliar to you, it would be well to inquire the best route and learn something about the building.
- Relax the night before the test – Allow your mind to rest. Do not study at all that night. Plan some mild recreation or diversion; then go to bed early and get a good night's sleep.
- Get up early enough to make a leisurely trip to the place for the test – This way unforeseen events, traffic snarls, unfamiliar buildings, etc. will not upset you.
- Dress comfortably – A written test is not a fashion show. You will be known by number and not by name, so wear something comfortable.

- Leave excess paraphernalia at home – Shopping bags and odd bundles will get in your way. You need bring only the items mentioned in the official notice you received; usually everything you need is provided. Do not bring reference books to the exam. They will only confuse those last minutes and be taken away from you when in the test room.
- Arrive somewhat ahead of time – If because of transportation schedules you must get there very early, bring a newspaper or magazine to take your mind off yourself while waiting.
- Locate the examination room – When you have found the proper room, you will be directed to the seat or part of the room where you will sit. Sometimes you are given a sheet of instructions to read while you are waiting. Do not fill out any forms until you are told to do so; just read them and be prepared.
- Relax and prepare to listen to the instructions
- If you have any physical problem that may keep you from doing your best, be sure to tell the test administrator. If you are sick or in poor health, you really cannot do your best on the exam. You can come back and take the test some other time.

VII. AT THE TEST

The day of the test is here and you have the test booklet in your hand. The temptation to get going is very strong. Caution! There is more to success than knowing the right answers. You must know how to identify your papers and understand variations in the type of short-answer question used in this particular examination. Follow these suggestions for maximum results from your efforts:

1) Cooperate with the monitor

The test administrator has a duty to create a situation in which you can be as much at ease as possible. He will give instructions, tell you when to begin, check to see that you are marking your answer sheet correctly, and so on. He is not there to guard you, although he will see that your competitors do not take unfair advantage. He wants to help you do your best.

2) Listen to all instructions

Don't jump the gun! Wait until you understand all directions. In most civil service tests you get more time than you need to answer the questions. So don't be in a hurry. Read each word of instructions until you clearly understand the meaning. Study the examples, listen to all announcements and follow directions. Ask questions if you do not understand what to do.

3) Identify your papers

Civil service exams are usually identified by number only. You will be assigned a number; you must not put your name on your test papers. Be sure to copy your number correctly. Since more than one exam may be given, copy your exact examination title.

4) Plan your time

Unless you are told that a test is a "speed" or "rate of work" test, speed itself is usually not important. Time enough to answer all the questions will be provided, but this does not mean that you have all day. An overall time limit has been set. Divide the total time (in minutes) by the number of questions to determine the approximate time you have for each question.

5) Do not linger over difficult questions

If you come across a difficult question, mark it with a paper clip (useful to have along) and come back to it when you have been through the booklet. One caution if you do this – be sure to skip a number on your answer sheet as well. Check often to be sure that you have not lost your place and that you are marking in the row numbered the same as the question you are answering.

6) Read the questions

Be sure you know what the question asks! Many capable people are unsuccessful because they failed to *read* the questions correctly.

7) Answer all questions

Unless you have been instructed that a penalty will be deducted for incorrect answers, it is better to guess than to omit a question.

8) Speed tests

It is often better NOT to guess on speed tests. It has been found that on timed tests people are tempted to spend the last few seconds before time is called in marking answers at random – without even reading them – in the hope of picking up a few extra points. To discourage this practice, the instructions may warn you that your score will be "corrected" for guessing. That is, a penalty will be applied. The incorrect answers will be deducted from the correct ones, or some other penalty formula will be used.

9) Review your answers

If you finish before time is called, go back to the questions you guessed or omitted to give them further thought. Review other answers if you have time.

10) Return your test materials

If you are ready to leave before others have finished or time is called, take ALL your materials to the monitor and leave quietly. Never take any test material with you. The monitor can discover whose papers are not complete, and taking a test booklet may be grounds for disqualification.

VIII. EXAMINATION TECHNIQUES

1) Read the general instructions carefully. These are usually printed on the first page of the exam booklet. As a rule, these instructions refer to the timing of the examination; the fact that you should not start work until the signal and must stop work at a signal, etc. If there are any *special* instructions, such as a choice of questions to be answered, make sure that you note this instruction carefully.

2) When you are ready to start work on the examination, that is as soon as the signal has been given, read the instructions to each question booklet, underline any key words or phrases, such as *least, best, outline, describe* and the like. In this way you will tend to answer as requested rather than discover on reviewing your paper that you *listed without describing*, that you selected the *worst* choice rather than the *best* choice, etc.

3) If the examination is of the objective or multiple-choice type – that is, each question will also give a series of possible answers: A, B, C or D, and you are called upon to select the best answer and write the letter next to that answer on your answer paper – it is advisable to start answering each question in turn. There may be anywhere from 50 to 100 such questions in the three or four hours allotted and you can see how much time would be taken if you read through all the questions before beginning to answer any. Furthermore, if you come across a question or group of questions which you know would be difficult to answer, it would undoubtedly affect your handling of all the other questions.

4) If the examination is of the essay type and contains but a few questions, it is a moot point as to whether you should read all the questions before starting to answer any one. Of course, if you are given a choice – say five out of seven and the like – then it is essential to read all the questions so you can eliminate the two that are most difficult. If, however, you are asked to answer all the questions, there may be danger in trying to answer the easiest one first because you may find that you will spend too much time on it. The best technique is to answer the first question, then proceed to the second, etc.

5) Time your answers. Before the exam begins, write down the time it started, then add the time allowed for the examination and write down the time it must be completed, then divide the time available somewhat as follows:
    - If 3-1/2 hours are allowed, that would be 210 minutes. If you have 80 objective-type questions, that would be an average of 2-1/2 minutes per question. Allow yourself no more than 2 minutes per question, or a total of 160 minutes, which will permit about 50 minutes to review.
    - If for the time allotment of 210 minutes there are 7 essay questions to answer, that would average about 30 minutes a question. Give yourself only 25 minutes per question so that you have about 35 minutes to review.

6) The most important instruction is to *read each question* and make sure you know what is wanted. The second most important instruction is to *time yourself properly* so that you answer every question. The third most important instruction is to *answer every question*. Guess if you have to but include something for each question. Remember that you will receive no credit for a blank and will probably receive some credit if you write something in answer to an essay question. If you guess a letter – say "B" for a multiple-choice question – you may have guessed right. If you leave a blank as an answer to a multiple-choice question, the examiners may respect your feelings but it will not add a point to your score. Some exams may penalize you for wrong answers, so in such cases *only*, you may not want to guess unless you have some basis for your answer.

7) Suggestions
    a. Objective-type questions
        1. Examine the question booklet for proper sequence of pages and questions
        2. Read all instructions carefully
        3. Skip any question which seems too difficult; return to it after all other questions have been answered
        4. Apportion your time properly; do not spend too much time on any single question or group of questions

5. Note and underline key words – *all, most, fewest, least, best, worst, same, opposite,* etc.
6. Pay particular attention to negatives
7. Note unusual option, e.g., unduly long, short, complex, different or similar in content to the body of the question
8. Observe the use of "hedging" words – *probably, may, most likely,* etc.
9. Make sure that your answer is put next to the same number as the question
10. Do not second-guess unless you have good reason to believe the second answer is definitely more correct
11. Cross out original answer if you decide another answer is more accurate; do not erase until you are ready to hand your paper in
12. Answer all questions; guess unless instructed otherwise
13. Leave time for review

   b. Essay questions
1. Read each question carefully
2. Determine exactly what is wanted. Underline key words or phrases.
3. Decide on outline or paragraph answer
4. Include many different points and elements unless asked to develop any one or two points or elements
5. Show impartiality by giving pros and cons unless directed to select one side only
6. Make and write down any assumptions you find necessary to answer the questions
7. Watch your English, grammar, punctuation and choice of words
8. Time your answers; don't crowd material

8) Answering the essay question

Most essay questions can be answered by framing the specific response around several key words or ideas. Here are a few such key words or ideas:

M's: manpower, materials, methods, money, management
P's: purpose, program, policy, plan, procedure, practice, problems, pitfalls, personnel, public relations

   a. Six basic steps in handling problems:
1. Preliminary plan and background development
2. Collect information, data and facts
3. Analyze and interpret information, data and facts
4. Analyze and develop solutions as well as make recommendations
5. Prepare report and sell recommendations
6. Install recommendations and follow up effectiveness

   b. Pitfalls to avoid
1. *Taking things for granted* – A statement of the situation does not necessarily imply that each of the elements is necessarily true; for example, a complaint may be invalid and biased so that all that can be taken for granted is that a complaint has been registered

2. *Considering only one side of a situation* – Wherever possible, indicate several alternatives and then point out the reasons you selected the best one
3. *Failing to indicate follow up* – Whenever your answer indicates action on your part, make certain that you will take proper follow-up action to see how successful your recommendations, procedures or actions turn out to be
4. *Taking too long in answering any single question* – Remember to time your answers properly

IX. AFTER THE TEST

Scoring procedures differ in detail among civil service jurisdictions although the general principles are the same. Whether the papers are hand-scored or graded by machine we have described, they are nearly always graded by number. That is, the person who marks the paper knows only the number – never the name – of the applicant. Not until all the papers have been graded will they be matched with names. If other tests, such as training and experience or oral interview ratings have been given, scores will be combined. Different parts of the examination usually have different weights. For example, the written test might count 60 percent of the final grade, and a rating of training and experience 40 percent. In many jurisdictions, veterans will have a certain number of points added to their grades.

After the final grade has been determined, the names are placed in grade order and an eligible list is established. There are various methods for resolving ties between those who get the same final grade – probably the most common is to place first the name of the person whose application was received first. Job offers are made from the eligible list in the order the names appear on it. You will be notified of your grade and your rank as soon as all these computations have been made. This will be done as rapidly as possible.

People who are found to meet the requirements in the announcement are called "eligibles." Their names are put on a list of eligible candidates. An eligible's chances of getting a job depend on how high he stands on this list and how fast agencies are filling jobs from the list.

When a job is to be filled from a list of eligibles, the agency asks for the names of people on the list of eligibles for that job. When the civil service commission receives this request, it sends to the agency the names of the three people highest on this list. Or, if the job to be filled has specialized requirements, the office sends the agency the names of the top three persons who meet these requirements from the general list.

The appointing officer makes a choice from among the three people whose names were sent to him. If the selected person accepts the appointment, the names of the others are put back on the list to be considered for future openings.

That is the rule in hiring from all kinds of eligible lists, whether they are for typist, carpenter, chemist, or something else. For every vacancy, the appointing officer has his choice of any one of the top three eligibles on the list. This explains why the person whose name is on top of the list sometimes does not get an appointment when some of the persons lower on the list do. If the appointing officer chooses the second or third eligible, the No. 1 eligible does not get a job at once, but stays on the list until he is appointed or the list is terminated.

X. HOW TO PASS THE INTERVIEW TEST

The examination for which you applied requires an oral interview test. You have already taken the written test and you are now being called for the interview test – the final part of the formal examination.

You may think that it is not possible to prepare for an interview test and that there are no procedures to follow during an interview. Our purpose is to point out some things you can do in advance that will help you and some good rules to follow and pitfalls to avoid while you are being interviewed.

What is an interview supposed to test?

The written examination is designed to test the technical knowledge and competence of the candidate; the oral is designed to evaluate intangible qualities, not readily measured otherwise, and to establish a list showing the relative fitness of each candidate – as measured against his competitors – for the position sought. Scoring is not on the basis of "right" and "wrong," but on a sliding scale of values ranging from "not passable" to "outstanding." As a matter of fact, it is possible to achieve a relatively low score without a single "incorrect" answer because of evident weakness in the qualities being measured.

Occasionally, an examination may consist entirely of an oral test – either an individual or a group oral. In such cases, information is sought concerning the technical knowledges and abilities of the candidate, since there has been no written examination for this purpose. More commonly, however, an oral test is used to supplement a written examination.

Who conducts interviews?

The composition of oral boards varies among different jurisdictions. In nearly all, a representative of the personnel department serves as chairman. One of the members of the board may be a representative of the department in which the candidate would work. In some cases, "outside experts" are used, and, frequently, a businessman or some other representative of the general public is asked to serve. Labor and management or other special groups may be represented. The aim is to secure the services of experts in the appropriate field.

However the board is composed, it is a good idea (and not at all improper or unethical) to ascertain in advance of the interview who the members are and what groups they represent. When you are introduced to them, you will have some idea of their backgrounds and interests, and at least you will not stutter and stammer over their names.

What should be done before the interview?

While knowledge about the board members is useful and takes some of the surprise element out of the interview, there is other preparation which is more substantive. It *is* possible to prepare for an oral interview – in several ways:

1) Keep a copy of your application and review it carefully before the interview

This may be the only document before the oral board, and the starting point of the interview. Know what education and experience you have listed there, and the sequence and dates of all of it. Sometimes the board will ask you to review the highlights of your experience for them; you should not have to hem and haw doing it.

2) Study the class specification and the examination announcement

Usually, the oral board has one or both of these to guide them. The qualities, characteristics or knowledges required by the position sought are stated in these documents. They offer valuable clues as to the nature of the oral interview. For example, if the job involves supervisory responsibilities, the announcement will usually indicate that knowledge of modern supervisory methods and the qualifications of the candidate as a supervisor will be tested. If so, you can expect such questions, frequently in the form of a hypothetical situation which you are expected to solve. NEVER go into an oral without knowledge of the duties and responsibilities of the job you seek.

3) Think through each qualification required

Try to visualize the kind of questions you would ask if you were a board member. How well could you answer them? Try especially to appraise your own knowledge and background in each area, *measured against the job sought*, and identify any areas in which you are weak. Be critical and realistic – do not flatter yourself.

4) Do some general reading in areas in which you feel you may be weak

For example, if the job involves supervision and your past experience has NOT, some general reading in supervisory methods and practices, particularly in the field of human relations, might be useful. Do NOT study agency procedures or detailed manuals. The oral board will be testing your understanding and capacity, not your memory.

5) Get a good night's sleep and watch your general health and mental attitude

You will want a clear head at the interview. Take care of a cold or any other minor ailment, and of course, no hangovers.

What should be done on the day of the interview?

Now comes the day of the interview itself. Give yourself plenty of time to get there. Plan to arrive somewhat ahead of the scheduled time, particularly if your appointment is in the fore part of the day. If a previous candidate fails to appear, the board might be ready for you a bit early. By early afternoon an oral board is almost invariably behind schedule if there are many candidates, and you may have to wait. Take along a book or magazine to read, or your application to review, but leave any extraneous material in the waiting room when you go in for your interview. In any event, relax and compose yourself.

The matter of dress is important. The board is forming impressions about you – from your experience, your manners, your attitude, and your appearance. Give your personal appearance careful attention. Dress your best, but not your flashiest. Choose conservative, appropriate clothing, and be sure it is immaculate. This is a business interview, and your appearance should indicate that you regard it as such. Besides, being well groomed and properly dressed will help boost your confidence.

Sooner or later, someone will call your name and escort you into the interview room. *This is it.* From here on you are on your own. It is too late for any more preparation. But remember, you asked for this opportunity to prove your fitness, and you are here because your request was granted.

What happens when you go in?

The usual sequence of events will be as follows: The clerk (who is often the board stenographer) will introduce you to the chairman of the oral board, who will introduce you to the other members of the board. Acknowledge the introductions before you sit down. Do not be surprised if you find a microphone facing you or a stenotypist sitting by. Oral interviews are usually recorded in the event of an appeal or other review.

Usually the chairman of the board will open the interview by reviewing the highlights of your education and work experience from your application – primarily for the benefit of the other members of the board, as well as to get the material into the record. Do not interrupt or comment unless there is an error or significant misinterpretation; if that is the case, do not hesitate. But do not quibble about insignificant matters. Also, he will usually ask you some question about your education, experience or your present job – partly to get you to start talking and to establish the interviewing "rapport." He may start the actual questioning, or turn it over to one of the other members. Frequently, each member undertakes the questioning on a particular area, one in which he is perhaps most competent, so you can expect each member to participate in the examination. Because time is limited, you may also expect some rather abrupt switches in the direction the questioning takes, so do not be upset by it. Normally, a board member will not pursue a single line of questioning unless he discovers a particular strength or weakness.

After each member has participated, the chairman will usually ask whether any member has any further questions, then will ask you if you have anything you wish to add. Unless you are expecting this question, it may floor you. Worse, it may start you off on an extended, extemporaneous speech. The board is not usually seeking more information. The question is principally to offer you a last opportunity to present further qualifications or to indicate that you have nothing to add. So, if you feel that a significant qualification or characteristic has been overlooked, it is proper to point it out in a sentence or so. Do not compliment the board on the thoroughness of their examination – they have been sketchy, and you know it. If you wish, merely say, "No thank you, I have nothing further to add." This is a point where you can "talk yourself out" of a good impression or fail to present an important bit of information. Remember, *you close the interview yourself*.

The chairman will then say, "That is all, Mr. _____, thank you." Do not be startled; the interview is over, and quicker than you think. Thank him, gather your belongings and take your leave. Save your sigh of relief for the other side of the door.

How to put your best foot forward

Throughout this entire process, you may feel that the board individually and collectively is trying to pierce your defenses, seek out your hidden weaknesses and embarrass and confuse you. Actually, this is not true. They are obliged to make an appraisal of your qualifications for the job you are seeking, and they want to see you in your best light. Remember, they must interview all candidates and a non-cooperative candidate may become a failure in spite of their best efforts to bring out his qualifications. Here are 15 suggestions that will help you:

1) Be natural – Keep your attitude confident, not cocky

If you are not confident that you can do the job, do not expect the board to be. Do not apologize for your weaknesses, try to bring out your strong points. The board is interested in a positive, not negative, presentation. Cockiness will antagonize any board member and make him wonder if you are covering up a weakness by a false show of strength.

2) Get comfortable, but don't lounge or sprawl

Sit erectly but not stiffly. A careless posture may lead the board to conclude that you are careless in other things, or at least that you are not impressed by the importance of the occasion. Either conclusion is natural, even if incorrect. Do not fuss with your clothing, a pencil or an ashtray. Your hands may occasionally be useful to emphasize a point; do not let them become a point of distraction.

3) Do not wisecrack or make small talk

This is a serious situation, and your attitude should show that you consider it as such. Further, the time of the board is limited – they do not want to waste it, and neither should you.

4) Do not exaggerate your experience or abilities

In the first place, from information in the application or other interviews and sources, the board may know more about you than you think. Secondly, you probably will not get away with it. An experienced board is rather adept at spotting such a situation, so do not take the chance.

5) If you know a board member, do not make a point of it, yet do not hide it

Certainly you are not fooling him, and probably not the other members of the board. Do not try to take advantage of your acquaintanceship – it will probably do you little good.

6) Do not dominate the interview

Let the board do that. They will give you the clues – do not assume that you have to do all the talking. Realize that the board has a number of questions to ask you, and do not try to take up all the interview time by showing off your extensive knowledge of the answer to the first one.

7) Be attentive

You only have 20 minutes or so, and you should keep your attention at its sharpest throughout. When a member is addressing a problem or question to you, give him your undivided attention. Address your reply principally to him, but do not exclude the other board members.

8) Do not interrupt

A board member may be stating a problem for you to analyze. He will ask you a question when the time comes. Let him state the problem, and wait for the question.

9) Make sure you understand the question

Do not try to answer until you are sure what the question is. If it is not clear, restate it in your own words or ask the board member to clarify it for you. However, do not haggle about minor elements.

10) Reply promptly but not hastily

A common entry on oral board rating sheets is "candidate responded readily," or "candidate hesitated in replies." Respond as promptly and quickly as you can, but do not jump to a hasty, ill-considered answer.

11) Do not be peremptory in your answers

A brief answer is proper – but do not fire your answer back. That is a losing game from your point of view. The board member can probably ask questions much faster than you can answer them.

12) Do not try to create the answer you think the board member wants

He is interested in what kind of mind you have and how it works – not in playing games. Furthermore, he can usually spot this practice and will actually grade you down on it.

13) Do not switch sides in your reply merely to agree with a board member

Frequently, a member will take a contrary position merely to draw you out and to see if you are willing and able to defend your point of view. Do not start a debate, yet do not surrender a good position. If a position is worth taking, it is worth defending.

14) Do not be afraid to admit an error in judgment if you are shown to be wrong

The board knows that you are forced to reply without any opportunity for careful consideration. Your answer may be demonstrably wrong. If so, admit it and get on with the interview.

15) Do not dwell at length on your present job

The opening question may relate to your present assignment. Answer the question but do not go into an extended discussion. You are being examined for a *new* job, not your present one. As a matter of fact, try to phrase ALL your answers in terms of the job for which you are being examined.

Basis of Rating

Probably you will forget most of these "do's" and "don'ts" when you walk into the oral interview room. Even remembering them all will not ensure you a passing grade. Perhaps you did not have the qualifications in the first place. But remembering them will help you to put your best foot forward, without treading on the toes of the board members.

Rumor and popular opinion to the contrary notwithstanding, an oral board wants you to make the best appearance possible. They know you are under pressure – but they also want to see how you respond to it as a guide to what your reaction would be under the pressures of the job you seek. They will be influenced by the degree of poise you display, the personal traits you show and the manner in which you respond.

ABOUT THIS BOOK

This book contains tests divided into Examination Sections. Go through each test, answering every question in the margin. We have also attached a sample answer sheet at the back of the book that can be removed and used. At the end of each test look at the answer key and check your answers. On the ones you got wrong, look at the right answer choice and learn. Do not fill in the answers first. Do not memorize the questions and answers, but understand the answer and principles involved. On your test, the questions will likely be different from the samples. Questions are changed and new ones added. If you understand these past questions you should have success with any changes that arise. Tests may consist of several types of questions. We have additional books on each subject should more study be advisable or necessary for you. Finally, the more you study, the better prepared you will be. This book is intended to be the last thing you study before you walk into the examination room. Prior study of relevant texts is also recommended. NLC publishes some of these in our Fundamental Series. Knowledge and good sense are important factors in passing your exam. Good luck also helps. So now study this Passbook, absorb the material contained within and take that knowledge into the examination. Then do your best to pass that exam.

EXAMINATION SECTION

EXAMINATION SECTION
TEST 1

DIRECTIONS: Each question or incomplete statement is followed by several suggested answers or completions. Select the one that BEST answers the question or completes the statement. *PRINT THE LETTER OF THE CORRECT ANSWER IN THE SPACE AT THE RIGHT.*

Questions 1-12.

DIRECTIONS: Questions 1 through 12 refer to the following information.

At the Supreme Plastic Company, located in Detroit, employees are paid bi-weekly. Their paychecks are calculated on the following deductions from their gross pay:

    a. Federal and State tax combined is 14%
    b. City tax of 3%, only for Detroit residents
    c. Union dues for union members only. The union dues are calculated as follows: 1.5% of an employee's gross pay or $15, <u>whichever is smaller</u>
    d. Medical coverage, which is calculated as follows: 2% of gross pay for employees under the age of 30, and 3.5% of gross pay for employees 30 years of age or older.

1. Charlie's gross pay per paycheck is $840. He lives outside Detroit, is not a union member, and is 36 years old.
What is his net pay?

    A. $680.40   B. $693.00   C. $705.60   D. $718.20   E. $730.80

2. Diane's gross pay per paycheck is $920. She lives in Detroit, is not a union member, and is 29 years old. What is her net pay?

    A. $782.00   B. $772.80   C. $763.60   D. $754.40   E. $745.20

3. Barney's gross pay per paycheck is $1030. He lives outside Detroit, is a union member, and is 25 years old. What is his net pay?

    A. $850.20   B. $857.70   C. $865.20   D. $872.70   E. $880.20

4. Vanessa's gross pay per paycheck is $980. She lives in Detroit, is a union member, and is 40 years old.
What is her net pay?

    A. $749.70   B. $757.05   C. $764.40   D. $771.75   E. $779.10

5. Fred's gross pay per paycheck is $750. He lives in Detroit, is a union member, and is 30 years old. What is his net pay?

    A. $607.50   B. $596.25   C. $585.00   D. $573.75   E. $562.50

6. Christine lives outside Detroit, is not a union member, and is 23 years old. Her net pay per paycheck is $567.00. What is her gross pay?

    A. $662.50   B. $675.00   C. $687.50   D. $700.00   E. $712.50

7. Marie lives in Detroit, is not a union member, and is 33 years old. Her net pay per paycheck is $890.40.
   What is her gross pay?

   A. $1060.00   B. $1080.00   C. $1100.00
   D. $1120.00   E. $1140.00

8. Todd lives outside Detroit, is a union member, and is 45 years old. His net pay per paycheck is $607.82.
   What is his gross pay?

   A. $779.60   B. $772.30   C. $765.00   D. $757.70   E. $750.40

9. Priscilla lives in Detroit, is a union member, and is 27 years old. Her net pay per paycheck is $981.46.
   What is her gross pay?

   A. $1246.80   B. $1238.50   C. $1230.20
   D. $1221.90   E. $1213.60

10. During the first two-week pay period in May, Floyd was a Detroit resident and not a union member. As of the second two-week pay period in May, he moved out of Detroit and joined the company union.
    If his gross pay per paycheck remained at $1300, how much was the *increase* in net pay?

    A. $15.00   B. $19.50   C. $24.00   D. $28.50   E. $33.00

11. During the first two-week pay period in July, Paula was not a Detroit resident, but was a union member. As of the second two-week pay period in July, she moved to Detroit and left the company union.
    If her gross pay per paycheck remained at $880, how much was the *decrease* in net pay?

    A. $9.60   B. $10.50   C. $11.40   D. $12.30   E. $13.20

12. Roger is a 50-year-old employee. During the first two-week pay period in August, he carried medical insurance. Due to financial hardship, he was allowed to drop this coverage as of the second two-week pay period. The net pay on his second paycheck was $18.92 higher than that of his first paycheck.
    What is his gross pay?

    A. $524.10   B. $529.60   C. $535.10   D. $540.60   E. $546.10

Questions 13-25.

DIRECTIONS: Questions 13 through 25 refer to the following information.

At the Lucky Star Restaurant, employees are paid weekly. Their paychecks are calculated on the following deductions from their gross pay (salary earnings):

   a. Federal and State tax combined is applied to salary earnings only (not including tips) in the following manner: 12% of salary up to and including a weekly salary of $400, plus 10% of any salary in excess of $400
   b. Tax on tips. This is calculated on <u>the larger of</u> $3 or 2% of tips collected.

c. Medical coverage, which is optional. The amount deducted is as shown in this chart:

Employee's Age (Yrs)	Employee's Years of Service		
	Less Than 1 Year	1-5 Years	Over 5 Years
18-30	$5	$4	$3
31-40	$9	$7	$5
Over 40	$13	$10	$7

NOTE: Net pay will include the tips earned, if the person involved did earn tips.

13. Frank's gross pay per paycheck is $380, including tips. In a particular week, he receives $50 in tips.
    If he has no medical coverage, what is his net pay?

    A. $387.40   B. $385.40   C. $383.40   D. $381.40   E. $379.40

14. Gina's gross pay per paycheck is $460, excluding tips. In a particular week, she receives $70 in tips.
    If she has no medical coverage, what is her net pay?

    A. $461.00   B. $467.00   C. $473.00   D. $479.00   E. $485.00

15. Cliff's gross pay per paycheck is $510, excluding tips. In a particular week, he receives $180 in tips.
    If he has no medical coverage, what is his net pay?

    A. $627.40   B. $638.00   C. $648.60   D. $659.20   E. $669.80

16. Diane's gross pay per paycheck is $350, excluding tips. In a particular week, she receives $200 in tips.
    If she has no medical coverage, what is her net pay?

    A. $506.00   B. $505.50   C. $505.00   D. $504.50   E. $504.00

17. Jean is a part-time cashier, earning a weekly salary of $320. She receives no tips, but does carry medical coverage.
    If she is 23 years old and has 4 years of service, what is her net pay?

    A. $275.60   B. $277.60   C. $279.60   D. $281.60   E. $283.60

18. Pete is a part-time cook, earning a weekly salary of $440. He receives no tips, but does carry medical coverage.
    If he is 42 years old and has 8 years of service, what is his net pay?

    A. $377.80   B. $378.60   C. $379.40   D. $380.20   E. $381.00

19. Melissa is a waitress, earning a weekly salary of $560, excluding tips. During one week, she receives $130 in tips.
    If she has medical coverage, is 36 years old, and has 5 years of service, what is her net pay?

    A. $613.00   B. $616.00   C. $619.00   D. $622.00   E. $625.00

20. Henry is a part-time waiter, earning a weekly salary of $350, excluding tips. During one week, he receives $90 in tips.
If he has medical coverage, is 32 years old, and has 7 months of service, what is his net pay?

   A. $386.00   B. $388.00   C. $390.00   D. $392.00   E. $394.00

21. During the first week of November, Roseanne was a waitress, earning a weekly salary of $570, plus $140 in tips. During the second week of November, her weekly salary was increased by 6% and her tips rose by 10%. What was her total net pay for these two weeks? (Assume no medical coverage for either week.)

   A. $1311.90   B. $1317.50   C. $1323.10
   D. $1328.70   E. $1334.30

22. During the first week of October, Don was a waiter, earning a weekly salary of $610, plus $100 in tips. He had no medical coverage at that time. During the second week of October, he was promoted to an Assistant Manager with a weekly salary of $800 and no tips. He also carried medical coverage. During that time frame, he had 4 years of service and was 52 years old.
What was his total net pay for these weeks?

   A. $1320.00   B. $1325.00   C. $1330.00
   D. $1335.00   E. $1340.00

23. Arlene is a waitress, 46 years old, with 10 months of service. During one particular week, she had $50 in tips and net pay of $305.04.
If she has medical coverage, what is her gross pay, excluding tips?

   A. $296.00   B. $302.00   C. $308.00   D. $314.00   E. $320.00

24. Francine is the restaurant's bookkeeper. She is 39 years old with 10 years of service. She carries medical coverage and her weekly salary includes no tips.
If her net pay per week is $869.45, what is her gross pay?

   A. $980.50   B. $978.10   C. $975.70   D. $973.30   E. $970.90

25. Ray is the chief waiter. He is 60 years old with 20 years of service. He carries medical coverage and his gross weekly salary, excluding tips, is $750. Assuming his weekly tips exceed $150, if his net pay (including salary and tips) is $934.40, how much does he earn in tips?

   A. $271.00   B. $274.00   C. $277.00   D. $280.00   E. $283.00

KEY (CORRECT ANSWERS)

1.	B	11.	E
2.	E	12.	D
3.	A	13.	D
4.	C	14.	C
5.	C	15.	A
6.	B	16.	E
7.	D	17.	B
8.	E	18.	E
9.	C	19.	B
10.	C	20.	A

21. D
22. E
23. C
24. A
25. D

SOLUTIONS TO PROBLEMS

1. CORRECT ANSWER: B
   Net pay = $840 - (.14)(840) - (.035)(840) = $693.00

2. CORRECT ANSWER: E
   Net pay = $920 - (.14)(920) - (.03)(920) - (.02)(920) = $745.20

3. CORRECT ANSWER: A
   Net pay = $1030 - (.14)(1030) - 15 - (.02)(1030) = $850.20

4. CORRECT ANSWER: C
   Net pay = $980 - (.14)(980) - (.03)(980) - (.015)(980) - (.035)(980) = $764.40

5. CORRECT ANSWER: C
   Net pay = $750 - (.14)(750) - (.03)(750) - (.015)(750) - (.035)(750) = $585.00

6. CORRECT ANSWER: B
   Let x = gross pay. Then, $x - .14x - .02x = \$567.00$
   Simplifying, $.84x = 567.00$, so $x - \$675.00$

7. CORRECT ANSWER: D
   Let x = gross pay. Then, $x - .14x - .03x - .035x = \$890.40$. Simplifying, $.795x = 890.40$, so $x = \$1120.00$

8. CORRECT ANSWER: E
   Let x = gross pay. Then, $x - .14x - .015x - .035x = \$607.82$. Simplifying, $.81x = 607.82$, so $x = \$750.40$

9. CORRECT ANSWER: C
   Let x = gross pay. Then, $x - .14x - .03x - \$15 - .02x = \$981.46$.
   Simplifying, $.81x = 996.46$, so $x = \$1230.20$. NOTE: Her union dues were $15, not 1.5% of her gross pay because 1.5% of 1230.20 is $18.45, which exceeds $15.

10. CORRECT ANSWER: C
    His net pay was affected by a $15 decrease due to union dues, but also by a (.03)($1300) = $39 increase due to moving out of Detroit. Finally, $39 - $15 = $24

11. CORRECT ANSWER: E
    Her net pay was affected by a (.015)($880) = $13.20 increase due to the removal of union dues, and also by a (.03)($880) = $26.40 decrease due to a Detroit city tax. Thus, her net pay was decreased by $26.40 - $13.20 = $13.20.

12. CORRECT ANSWER: D
    His medical coverage represents 3.5% of his gross pay. If his gross pay = x, then $.035x = \$18.92$. Solving, x $540.60

13. CORRECT ANSWER: D
    Net pay = $430 - (.12)(380) - 3 = $331.40

14. CORRECT ANSWER: C
    Net pay = $530 - (.12)(400) - (.10)(60) - 3 = $473.00

15. CORRECT ANSWER: A
    Net pay = $690 - (.12)(400) - (.10)(110) - (.02)(180) = $627.40

16. CORRECT ANSWER: E
    Net pay = $550 - (.12)(350) - (.02)(200) = $504.00

17. CORRECT ANSWER: B
    Net pay = $320 - (.12)(320) - 4 = $277.60

18. CORRECT ANSWER: E
    Net pay = $440 - (.12)(400) - (.10)(40) - 7 = $381.00

19. CORRECT ANSWER: B
    Net pay = $690 - (.12)(400) - (.10)(160) - 3 - 7 = $486.00

20. CORRECT ANSWER: A
    Net pay = $440 - (.12)(350) - 3 - 9 = $386.00

21. CORRECT ANSWER: D
    First week net pay = $710 - (.12)(400) - (.10)(170) - 3 = $642.00
    Second week net pay = $758.20 - (.12)(400) - (.10)(204.20) - (154)(.02) = $686.70
    Total net pay = $1328.70

22. CORRECT ANSWER: E
    First week net pay = $710 - (.12)(400) - (.10)(210) - 3 = $638.00
    Second week net pay = $800 - (.12)(400) - (.10)(400) - 10 = $702.00
    Total net pay = $1340.00

23. CORRECT ANSWER: C
    Let x = gross pay, excluding tips. Then, we have: x + 50 - .12x - 3 - 13 = $305.04. This simplifes to .88x = 271.04.
    Solving, x - $308.00

24. CORRECT ANSWER: A
    Let x = gross pay. Then, x - (.12)(400) - (.10)(x-400) - 5 = $869.45. Simplifying, x - 48 - .10x + 40 - 5 = 869.45. Then, .90x = 882.45.
    Solving, x - $980.50

25. CORRECT ANSWER: D
    Let x = tips earned. Then, $750 + x - (400)(.12) - (350)(.10) - .02x - 7 = 934.40.
    Simplifying, .98x + 660 = 934.40.
    Solving, x = $280.00

TEST 2

DIRECTIONS: Each question or incomplete statement is followed by several suggested answers or completions. Select the one that BEST answers the question or completes the statement. *PRINT THE LETTER OF THE CORRECT ANSWER IN THE SPACE AT THE RIGHT.*

Questions 1-13.

DIRECTIONS: Questions 1 through 13 refer to the following information.

At the Stretch-Tight Rubber Band Company, employees are paid on the 15th day and the last day of every month. Their paychecks are calculated based on the following deductions from their gross pay:

a. Federal tax of 12%
b. State tax of 7%
c. Union dues for union members only. The union dues are calculated as follows: .5% for up to 1 year of employment; 1% for more than 1 year but no more than 5 years of employment; 1.5% for more than 5 years of employment.

1. Jack's gross pay per paycheck is $1000. If he is NOT a union member, what is his net pay?

    A. $930   B. $880   C. $810   D. $720   E. $640

2. Robin's gross pay per paycheck is $900. If she is a union member with 3 years of employment, what is her net pay?

    A. $720   B. $729   C. $738   D. $747   E. $756

3. Suzanne's gross pay per paycheck is $1200. If she is a union member with 6 years of employment, what is her net pay?

    A. $1008   B. $990   C. $972   D. $954   E. $936

4. Mike's gross pay per paycheck is $1600. If he is a union member with 5 months of employment, what is his net pay?

    A. $1240   B. $1248   C. $1264   D. $1280   E. $1288

5. For the month of May, Bonnie was not a union member up through May 15th, but became a union member on May 16th. She has 8 years of employment, and her gross pay per paycheck is $860.
   What is her TOTAL net pay for May?

    A. $1347.50   B. $1354.10   C. $1367.40
    D. $1380.30   E. $1393.20

6. For the month of June, Bob was not a union member up through June 15th, but became a union member on June 16th. He has 4 years of employment, and his gross pay per paycheck is $700.
   What is his TOTAL net pay for June?

    A. $1135   B. $1127   C. $1120   D. $1112   E. $1104

7. Alice is not a union member and her net pay per paycheck is $761.40. What is her gross pay?

   A. $860   B. $900   C. $940   D. $1000   E. $1060

8. Paul is a union member with 3 months of employment. If his net pay per paycheck is $627.90, what is his gross pay?

   A. $760   B. $765   C. $770   D. $775   E. $780

9. Linda is a union member with 7 years of employment. If her net pay per paycheck is $898.35, what is her gross pay?

   A. $1130   B. $1140   C. $1150   D. $1160   E. $1170

10. Ralph is a union member with 2 years of employment. If his net pay per paycheck is $1136, what is his gross pay?

    A. $1438   B. $1420   C. $1410   D. $1402   E. $1388

11. Mary is a union member, and at the end of July of this year, she will have completed 1 year of employment. Her gross pay per paycheck in July is $1050, but beginning in August her gross pay (per paycheck) will become $1180.
    What will be the *increase* in her net pay from July to August?

    A. $86.40   B. $98.75   C. $112.45   D. $130.00   E. $143.35

12. Steve is a union member, and at the end of March of this year, he will have completed 5 years of employment. His gross pay per paycheck in March is $980, but beginning in April his gross pay (per paycheck) will become $1100.
    What will be the *increase* in his net pay from March to April?

    A. $62.50   B. $73.00   C. $84.50   D. $90.50   E. $96.00

13. Sherry has been a union member up through September of this year. She has 8 months of employment, and her gross pay per paycheck is $800. Beginning in October, she will become a non-union member, and her gross pay (per paycheck) will drop to $660.
    What will be the *decrease* in her net pay from September to October?

    A. $109.40   B. $110.80   C. $112.70   D. $113.40   E. $115.60

Questions 14-25.

DIRECTIONS: Questions 14 through 25 refer to the following information.

At the Iron-Clad Steel Company, employees are paid weekly. Their paychecks are calculated based on the following deductions from their gross pay:

   a. Federal tax and State tax combined is 16%
   b. Union dues for union members only. The union dues are calculated as follows: 2% of an employee's gross pay, up to and including a gross pay of $500, plus of any gross pay in excess of $500.
   c. Medical coverage, which is calculated as follows, based on the employee's age: 1.5% of gross pay for employees age 18 through 25; 2.5% of gross pay for employees age 26 through 39; and 5% for employees age 40 or older.

14. Bill's gross pay per paycheck is $820. If he is 24 years old and is not a union member, what is his net pay?   14.____

    A. $651.90   B. $664.20   C. $676.50   D. $688.80   E. $701.10

15. Debra's gross pay per paycheck is $740. If she is 41 years old and is not a union member, what is her net pay?   15.____

    A. $620.40   B. $602.50   C. $584.60   D. $566.70   E. $548.80

16. Mark's gross pay per paycheck is $700. If he is 32 years old and a union member, what is his net pay?   16.____

    A. $564.50   B. $562.50   C. $560.50   D. $558.50   E. $556.50

17. Virginia's gross pay per paycheck is $490. If she is 19 years old and a union member, what is her net pay?   17.____

    A. $378.85   B. $382.75   C. $386.65   D. $390.55   E. $394.45

18. Rhonda's gross pay per paycheck is $650. If she is 45 years old and a union member, what is her net pay?   18.____

    A. $485.75   B. $502.00   C. $518.25   D. $534.50   E. $550.75

19. For the first week in June, Marianne was not a union member, but became a union member at the beginning of the second week. Her gross pay per paycheck is $880, and she is 38 years old.   19.____
    What is her TOTAL net pay for these two weeks?

    A. $1448.20   B. $1441.30   C. $1434.40
    D. $1427.50   E. $1420.60

20. For the first week in January, Carl was not a union member, but became a union member at the beginning of the second week. His gross pay per paycheck is $470, and he is 22 years old.   20.____
    What is his TOTAL net pay for these two weeks?

    A. $766.10   B. $775.50   C. $784.90   D. $794.30   E. $803.70

21. Dave's gross pay per paycheck during the first week of October was $450, but his gross pay increased to $550 for the second week in October. If he is 50 years old and a union member, what is his TOTAL net pay for these two weeks?   21.____

    A. $805.00   B. $793.50   C. $782.00   D. $770.50   E. $759.00

22. Nancy is not a union member and her net pay per paycheck is $513.45. If she is 35 years old, what is her gross pay?   22.____

    A. $615   B. $620   C. $625   D. $630   E. $635

23. Phyllis is not a union member and her net pay per paycheck is $639.90. If she is 43 years old, what is her gross pay?   23.____

    A. $780   B. $795   C. $810   D. $825   E. $840

24. Tom is a union member and his net pay per paycheck is $350.90. If he is 21 years old, what is his gross pay?   24.____

   A. $436   B. $448   C. $460   D. $472   E. $484

25. Ron is a union member and his net pay per paycheck is $767.80. If he is 37 years old, what is his gross pay?   25.____

   A. $972.50   B. $960.00   C. $947.50   D. $935.00   E. $922.50

KEY (CORRECT ANSWERS)

1. C	11. B
2. A	12. D
3. D	13. A
4. E	14. C
5. D	15. C
6. B	16. D
7. C	17. E
8. E	18. B
9. A	19. E
10. B	20. A

21. D
22. D
23. C
24. A
25. B

SOLUTIONS TO PROBLEMS

1. CORRECT ANSWER: C
   Net pay = $1000 - (.12)(1000) - (.07)(1000) = $810

2. CORRECT ANSWER: A
   Net pay = $900 - (.12)(900) - (.07)(900) - (.01)(900) = $720

3. CORRECT ANSWER: D
   Net pay = $1200 - (.12)(1200) - (.07)(1200) - (.015)(1200) = $954

4. CORRECT ANSWER: E
   Net pay = $1600 - (.12)(1600) - (.07)(1600) - (.005)(1600) = $1288

5. CORRECT ANSWER: D
   Net pay = [$860 - (.12)(860) - (.07)(860)] + [$860 - (.12)(860) - (.07)(860) - (.015)(860)] = $1380.30

6. CORRECT ANSWER: B
   Net pay = [$700 - (.12)(700) - (.07)(700)] + [$700 - (.12)(700) - (.07)(700) - (.01)(700)] = $1127

7. CORRECT ANSWER: C
   Let x - gross pay. Then, x - .12x - .07x = 761.40, so .81x = 761.40. Solving, x = $940

8. CORRECT ANSWER: E
   Let x = gross pay. Then, x - .12x - .07x - .005x = 627.90
   So, .805x = 627.90. Solving, x = $780

9. CORRECT ANSWER: A
   Let x = gross pay. Then, x - .12x - .07x - .015x = 898.35,
   So .795x = 898.35.
   Solving, x $1130

10. CORRECT ANSWER: B
    Let x = gross pay. Then, x - .12x - .07x - .01x = 1136
    So, .80x = 1136. Solving, x = $1420

11. CORRECT ANSWER: B
    Mary's net pay in July = $1050 - (.12)(1050) - (.07)(1050) - (.005)(1050) = $845.25. Her net pay in August = $1180 -(.12)(1180) - (.07)(1180) - (.01)(1180) = $944.00
    Then, $944.00 - $845.25 = $98.75

12. CORRECT ANSWER: D
    Steve's net pay in March = $980 - (.12)(980) - (.07)(980)
    - (.01)(980) = 784.00. His net pay in April = $1100 - (.12)(1100)
    - (.07)(1100) - (.015)(1100) = $874.50. Then, $874.50 -$784.00 = $90.50

6 (#2)

13. CORRECT ANSWER: A
Sherry's net pay in September = $800 - (.12)(800) - (.07)(800) - (.005)(800) - $644.00. Her net pay in October = $660 -(.12)(660) - (.07)(660) = $534.60. Then, $644.00 - $534.60 = $109.40

14. CORRECT ANSWER: C
Net pay = $820 - (.16)(820) - (.015)(820) = $676.50

15. CORRECT ANSWER: C
Net pay = $740 - (.16)(740) - (.05)(740) = $584.60

16. CORRECT ANSWER: D
Net pay = $700 - (.16)(700) - (.02)(500) - (.01)(200) -(.025)(700) = $558.50

17. CORRECT ANSWER: E
Net pay = $490 - (.16)(490) - (.02)(490) - (.015)(490) = $394.45

18. CORRECT ANSWER: B
Net pay = $650 - (.16)(650) - (.02)(500) - (.01)(150). -(.05)(650) = $502.00

19. CORRECT ANSWER: E
Net pay = [$880 - (.16)(880) - (.025)(880)] + [$880 - (.16)(880) - (.02)(500) - (.01)(380) - (.025)(880)] = $1420.60

20. CORRECT ANSWER: A
Net pay = [$470 - (.16)(470) - (.015)(470)] + [$470 - (.16)(470) - (.02)(470) - (.015)(470)] = $766.10

21. CORRECT ANSWER: D
Net pay = [$450 - (.16)(450) - (.02)(450) - (.05)(450)] + [$550 - (.16)(550) - (.02)(500) - (.01)(50) - (.05)(550)] = $770.50

22. CORRECT ANSWER: D
Let x - gross pay. Then, x - .16x - .025x = 513.45, so, .815x = 513.45. Solving, x = $630

23. CORRECT ANSWER: C
Let x = gross pay. Then, x - .16x - .05x = 639.90, so .79x - 639.90. Solving, x = $810

24. CORRECT ANSWER: A
Let x = gross pay. We can safely assume that his gross pay is less than $500, since all five selections are under $500. Then, x - .16x - .02x - .015x = 350.98, so, .805x = 350.98. Solving, x = $436

25. CORRECT ANSWER: B
Let x = gross pay. Since his gross pay must exceed $500, x - .16x - (.02) (500) - (.01)(x-500) - .025x = 767.80. Simplifying, .805x - 5 - 767.80. Solving, x - $960.00

EXAMINATION SECTION
TEST 1

DIRECTIONS: Each question or incomplete statement is followed by several suggested answers or completions. Select the one that BEST answers the question or completes the statement. *PRINT THE LETTER OF THE CORRECT ANSWER IN THE SPACE AT THE RIGHT.*

1. The processing of payroll changes and the preparation of salary checks is done by the

    A. agency payroll unit
    B. Department of Audit and Control
    C. Department of Civil Service
    D. Office of General Services

2. Of the following, a *special payroll*

    A. is prepared during the period in which the employee is actually earning the money
    B. would need the approval of the Office of General Services
    C. would involve temporary employees
    D. would not be processed by a computer

3. Form PR-75 would be used to request

    A. a change in an employee's name
    B. overtime pay for a unit
    C. a job audit
    D. a reclassification for an employee

4. In setting due dates, DAY 14 of the payroll period in state agencies is

    A. Friday   B. Thursday
    C. Wednesday   D. Tuesday

5. In filling out a PR-75, if an employee _____, it would require a Group II classification.

    A. retires
    B. works overtime
    C. is reclassified
    D. receives a raise over $1,500 annually

6. In filling out a PR-75, if an employee _____, it would require a Group I classification.

    A. retires
    B. works overtime
    C. successfully completes a probationary period
    D. takes military leave without pay

7. Of the following, which deduction would NOT be directly handled by most agency payroll units?

    A. Credit union deductions   B. Fixed federal tax
    C. Federated funds   D. State health insurance

8. If, after percentage deductions, the employee's salary is insufficient to cover all fixed deductions, which of the following deductions should be eliminated before the others?

   A. Bonds
   B. Credit union
   C. Taxable maintenance
   D. Social Security adjustment

9. A reallocation is

   A. a change in an existing title
   B. a change of status from one classification to the next
   C. another term for transfer of an employee
   D. a change in the grade of an existing title with no change in the title

10. An employee's annual salary is $23,600. The biweekly factor based on a 365-day year is .038356.
    The employee's biweekly rate would be

    A. $885.90   B. $905.20   C. $615.28   D. $963.10

11. An employee's annual salary is $25,000. The employee is paid for 8 days in a biweekly period of 10 hour days for a 366-day year. The biweekly factor is .038251, and the work day factor is .125.
    What is the employee's work day rate?

    A. $111.56   B. $956   C. $119.54   D. $116.28

12. An employee has an annual salary of $13,850. There is a lump sum payment owed to the employee for accured credits totaling 6 days. The biweekly factor is .038356, and the work day rate is .10.
    The employee should receive a lump sum payment of

    A. $531.23   B. $318.74   C. $391.14   D. $481.15

13. An employee has an annual salary of $15,860. The biweekly factor is .048761, and the work day rate is .125. The employee's work day rate would be

    A. $96.73   B. $89.45   C. $98.64   D. $92.55

14. An employee's biweekly rate is $567.67. The hourly overtime rate is paid by the following formula: Annual Salary x .00075. The biweekly factor is .038356.
    If the employee works 8 hours of overtime, how much money will he have earned for the overtime?

    A. $148.00   B. $42.58   C. $88.80   D. $96.50

15. An employee is paid on a biweekly basis over 21 biweekly pay periods. The employee's annual salary is $19,500. The biweekly factor is .047619, and the calendar day factor is .0714286.
    Approximately what is her calendar day rate?

    A. $66.33   B. $92.86   C. $78.54   D. $73.58

KEY (CORRECT ANSWERS)

1. B
2. C
3. A
4. C
5. A

6. C
7. D
8. A
9. D
10. B

11. C
12. B
13. A
14. C
15. A

EXAMINATION SECTION

TEST 1

DIRECTIONS: Each question or incomplete statement is followed by several suggested answers or completions. Select the one that BEST answers the question or completes the statement. *PRINT THE LETTER OF THE CORRECT ANSWER IN THE SPACE AT THE RIGHT.*

Questions 1-5.

DIRECTIONS: Questions 1 through 5 are to be answered on the basis of the extracts from Federal income tax withholding and Social Security tax tables shown below. These tables indicate the amounts which must be withheld from the employee's salary by his employer for Federal income tax and for Social Security. They are based on weekly earnings.

INCOME TAX WITHHOLDING TABLE							
The wages are		And the number of withholding allowances is					
At Least	But Less Than	5	6	7	8	9	10 or More
		The amount of income tax to be withheld shall be					
$300	$320	$24.60	$19.00	$13.80	$ 8.60	$4.00	$ 0
320	340	28.80	22.80	17.40	12.20	7.00	2.80
340	360	33.00	27.00	21.00	15.80	10.60	5.60
360	380	37.20	31.20	25.20	19.40	14.20	9.00
380	400	41.40	34.40	29.40	23.40	17.80	12.60
400	420	45.60	39.60	33.60	27.60	21.40	16.20
420	440	49.80	43.80	37.80	31.80	25.60	19.80
440	460	54.00	48.00	42.00	36.00	29.80	23.80
460	480	58.20	52.20	46.20	40.20	34.00	38.00
480	500	62.40	46.40	40.40	44.40	38.20	32.20

SOCIAL SECURITY TABLE				
WAGES		Tax to be Withheld	WAGES		Tax to be Withheld
At Least	But Less Than		At Least	But Less Than	
$333.18	$333.52	$19.50	$336.60	$336.94	$19.70
333.52	333.86	19.52	336.94	337.28	19.72
333.86	334.20	19.54	337.28	337.62	19.74
334.20	334.54	19.56	337.62	337.96	19.76
334.54	334.88	19.58	337.96	338.30	19.78
334.88	335.22	19.60	338.30	338.64	19.80
335.22	335.56	19.62	338.64	338.98	19.82
335.56	335.90	19.64	338.98	339.32	19.84
335.90	336.24	19.66	339.32	339.66	19.86
336.24	336.60	19.68	339.66	340.00	19.88

1. If an employee has a weekly wage of $379.50 and claims 6 withholding allowances, the amount of income tax to be withheld is
   A. $27.00   B. $31.20   C. $35.40   D. $37.20

2. An employee had wages of $335.60 for one week.
   With eight withholding allowances claimed, how much income tax will be withheld from his salary?
   A. $8.60   B. $12.00   C. $13.80   D. $17.40

3. How much social security tax will an employee with weekly wages of $335.60 pay?
   A. $19.60   B. $19.62   C. $19.64   D. $19.66

4. Mr. Wise earns $339.80 a week and claims seven withholding allowances.
   What is his take-home pay after income tax and social security tax are deducted?
   A. $300.32   B. $302.52   C. $319.92   D. $322.40

5. If an employee pays $19.74 in social security tax and claims eight withholding allowances, the amount of income tax that should be withheld from his wages is
   A. $8.60   B. $12.20   C. $13.80   D. $15.80

6. A fundamental rule of bookkeeping states that an individual's assets equal his liabilities plus his proprietorship (ASSETS = LIABILITIES – PROPRIETORSHIP). Which of the following statements logically follows from this rule?
   A. ASSETS = PROPRIETORSHIP – LIABILITIES
   B. LIABILITIES = ASSETS + PROPRIETORSHIP
   C. PROPRIETORSHIP = ASSETS – LIABILITIES
   D. PROPRIETORSHIP = LIABILITIES + ASSETS

7. Mr. Martin's assets consist of the following:
   Cash on Hand: $5,233.74
   Furniture: $4,925.00
   Government Bonds: $5,500.00
   What are his TOTAL assets?
   A. $10,158.74 $10,425.00   C. $10,733.74   D. $15,658.74

8. If Mr. Mitchell has $627.04 in his checking account and then writes three checks for $241.74, $13.24, and $101.97, what will be his new balance?
   A. $257.88   B. $269.08   C. $357.96   D. $368.96

9. An employee's net pay is equal to his total earnings less all deductions.
   If an employee's total earnings in a pay period are $497.05, what is his NET pay if he has the following deductions: Federal income tax, $90.32; FICA: $28.74; State tax: $18.79; City tax: $7.25; Pension: $1.88?
   A. $351.17   B. $351.07   C. $350.17   D. $350.07

10. A petty cash fund had an opening balance of $85.75 on December 1.   10.____
Expenditures of $23.00, $15.65, $5.23, $14.75, and $26.38 were made out of his fund during the first 14 days of the month. Then, on December 17, another $38.50 was added to the fund.
If additional expenditures of $17.18, $3.29, and $11.64 were made during the remainder of the month, what was the FINAL balance of the petty cash fund at the end of December?
  A. $6.93   B. $7.13   C. $46.51   D. $91.40

Questions 11-15.

DIRECTIONS: Questions 11 through 15 are to be answered on the basis of the following instructions.

The chart below is used by the loan division of a city retirement system for the following purposes: (1) to calculate the monthly payment a member must pay on an outstanding loan; (2) to calculate how much a member owes on an outstanding loan after he has made a number of payments.

To calculate the amount a member must pay each month in repaying his loan, look at Column II on the chart. You will notice that each entry in Column II corresponds to a number appearing under the *Months* column; for example, 1.004868 corresponds to 1 month, 0.503654 corresponds to 2 months, etc. To calculate the amount a member must pay each month, use the following procedure: multiply the amount of the load by the entry in Column II which corresponds to the number of months over which the load will be paid back. For example, if a loan of $200 is taken out for six months, multiply $200 by 0.169518, the entry in Column II which corresponds to six months.

In order to calculate the balance still owed on an outstanding loan, multiply the monthly payment by the number in Column I which corresponds to the number of monthly payments which remain to be paid on the loan. For example, if a member is supposed to pay $106.00 a month for twelve months, after seven payments, five monthly payments remain. To calculate the balance owed on the loan at this point, multiply the $106.00 monthly payment by 4.927807, the number in Column I that corresponds to five months.

Months	Column I	Column II
1	0.995156	1.004868
2	1.985491	0.503654
3	2.971029	0.336584
4	3.951793	0.253050
5	4.927807	0.202930
6	5.899092	0.169518
7	6.865673	0.145652
8	7.827572	0.127754
9	8.784811	0.113833
10	9.737414	0.102697
11	10.685402	0.093586
12	11.628798	0.085994
13	12.567624	0.079570
14	13.501902	0.074064
15	14.431655	0.069292

11. If Mr. Carson borrows $1,500 for eight months, how much will he have to pay back each month?
    A. $187.16   B. $191.63   C. $208.72   D. $218.65

12. If a member borrows $2,400 for one year, the amount he will have to pay back each month is
    A. $118.78   B. $196.18   C. $202.28   D. $206.38

13. Mr. Elliott borrowed $1,700 for a period of fifteen months. Each month he will have to pay back
    A. $117.80   B. $116.96   C. $107.79   D. $101.79

14. Mr. Aylward is paying back a thirteen-month loan at the rate of $173.13 a month.
    If he has already made six monthly payments, how much does he owe on the outstanding loan?
    A. $1,027.38   B. $1,178.75   C. $1,188.65   D. $1,898.85

15. A loan was taken out for 15 months, and the monthly payment was $104.75. After two monthly payments, how much was still owed on this load?
    A. $515.79   B. $863.89   C. $1,116.76   D. $1,316.46

16. The ABC Corporation had a gross income of $125,500.00 in 2015. Of this, it paid 60% for overhead.
    If the gross income for 2016 increased by $6,500 and the cost of overhead increased to 61% of gross income, how much more did it pay for overhead in 2016 than in 2015?
    A. $1,320   B. $5,220   C. $7,530   D. $8,052

17. After one year, Mr. Richards paid back a total of $1,695.00 as payment for a $1,500.00 loan. All the money paid over $1,500.00 was simple interest. The interest charge was MOST NEARLY
    A. 13%   B. 11%   C. 9%   D. 7%

18. A checking account has a balance of $253.36.
    If deposits of $36.95, $210.23, and $7.34 and withdrawals of $117.35, $23.37, and $15.98 are made, what is the NEW balance of the account?
    A. $155.54   B. $351.18   C. $364.58   D. $664.58

19. In 2015, the W Realty Company spent 27% of its income on rent.
    If it earned $97,254.00 in 2015, the amount it paid for rent was
    A. $26.258.58   B. $26,348.58   C. $27,248.58   D. $27,358.58

20. Six percent simple annual interest on $2,436.18 is MOST NEARLY
    A. $145.08   B. $145.17   c. $146.08   D. $146.17

21. Assume that the XYZ Company has $10,402.72 cash on hand.
    If it pays $699.83 of this for rent, the amount of cash on hand would be
    A. $9,792.89   B. $9,702.89   C. $9,692.89   D. $9,602.89

22. On January 31, Mr. Warren's checking account had a balance of $933.68.
    If he deposited $36.40 on February 2, $126.00 on February 9, and $90.02 on February 16 and wrote no checks during this period, what was the balance of his account on February 17?
    A. $680.26   B. $681.26   C. $1,186.10   D. $1,187.00

23. Multiplying a number by .75 is the same as
    A. multiplying it by 2/3   B. dividing it by 2/3
    C. multiplying it by 3/4   D. dividing it by 3/4

24. In City Agency A, 2/3 of the employees are enrolled in a retirement system. City Agency B has the same number of employees as Agency A, and 60% of these are enrolled in a retirement system.
    If Agency A has a total of 660 employees, how many MORE employees does it have enrolled in a retirement system than does Agency B?
    B. 36   B. 44   C. 56   D. 66

25. Net Worth is equal to Assets minus Liabilities.
    If, at the end of year, a textile company had assets of $98,695.83 and liabilities of $59,238.29, what was its net worth?
    A. $38,478.54   B. $38,488.64   C. $39,457.54   D. $48,557.54

KEY (CORRECT ANSWERS)

1.	B	11.	B
2.	B	12.	D
3.	C	13.	A
4.	B	14.	C
5.	B	15.	D
6.	C	16.	B
7.	D	17.	A
8.	B	18.	B
9.	D	19.	A
10.	B	20.	D

21. B
22. C
23. C
24. B
25. C

TEST 2

DIRECTIONS: Each question or incomplete statement is followed by several suggested answers or completions. Select the one that BEST answers the question or completes the statement. *PRINT THE LETTER OF THE CORRECT ANSWER IN THE SPACE AT THE RIGHT.*

Questions 1-10.

DIRECTIONS: Questions 1 through 10 below present the identification numbers, initials, and last names of employees enrolled in a city retirement system. You are to choose the option (A, B, C, or D) that has the IDENTICAL identification number, initials, and last name as those given in each question.

<u>Sample Question</u>
B145698 JL Jones
    A.   B146798 JL Jones   B. B145698 JL Jonas
    C.   P145698 JL Jones   D. B145698 JL Jones

The correct answer is D. Only Option D shows the identification number, initials, and last name exactly as they are in the sample question. Options A, B, and C have errors in the identification number or last name.

1. J297483 PL Robinson
    A. J294783 PL Robinson   B. J297483 PL Robinson
    C. J297483 Pl Robinson   D. J297843 PL Robinson

1.____

2. S497662 JG Schwartz
    B.   S497662 JG Schwarz   B. S497762 JG Schwartz
    C.   S497662 JG Schwartz   D. S497663 JG Schwartz

2.____

3. G696436 LN Alberton
    A. G696436 LM Alberton   B. G696436 LN Albertson
    C. G696346 LN Albertson   D. G696436 LN Alberton

3.____

4. R774923 AD Aldrich
    A. R774923 AD Aldrich   B. R744923 AD Aldrich
    C. R774932 AP Aldrich   D. R774932 AD Allrich

4.____

5. N239638 RP Hrynyk
    A. N236938 PR Hrynyk   B. N236938 RP Hrynyk
    C. N239638 PR Hrynyk   D. N239638 Hrynyk

5.____

6. R156949 LT Carlson
    A. R156949 LT Carlton   B. R156494 LT Carlson
    C. R159649 LT Carlton   D. R156949 LT Carlson

6.____

7. T524697 MN Orenstein
    A. T524697 MN Orenstein   B. T524967 MN Orinstein
    C. T524697 NM Ornstein   D. T524967 NM Orenstein

7.____

25

8. L346239 JD Remsen
   A. L346239 JD Remson
   B. L364239 JD Remsen
   C. L346329 JD Remsen
   D. L346239 JD Remsen

9. P966438 SB Rieperson
   A. P996438 SB Rieperson
   B. P466438 SB Reiperson
   C. R996438 SB Rieperson
   D. P966438 SB Rieperson

10. D749382 CD Thompson
    A. P749382 CD Thompson
    B. D749832 CD Thomsonn
    C. D749382 CD Thompson
    D. D749823 CD Thomspon

Questions 11-20.

DIRECTIONS: Assume that each of the capital letters in the table below represents the name of an employee enrolled in the city's employees' personnel system. The number directly beneath the letter represents the agency for which the employee works, and the small letter directly beneath represents the code for the employee's account.

Name of Employee	L	O	T	Q	A	M	R	N	C
Agency	3	4	5	9	8	7	2	1	6
Account Code	r	f	b	i	d	t	g	e	n

In each of the following Questions 11 through 20, the agency code numbers and the account code letters in Columns 2 and 3 should correspond to the capital letters in Column 1 and should be in the same consecutive order. For each question, look at each column carefully and mark your answer as follows:

If there are one or more errors in Column 2 only, mark your answer A.
If there are one or more errors in Column 3 only, mark your answer B.
I there are one or more errors in Column 2 and one or more errors in Column 3, mark your answer C.
If there are NO errors in either column, mark your answer D.

Sample Question

Column 1   Column 2   Column 3
TQLMOC   583746   birtfn

In Column 2, the second agency code number (corresponding to letter Q) should be 9, not 8. Column 3 is coded correctly to Column 1. Since there is an error only in Column 2, the correct answer is A.

	COLUMN 1	COLUMN 2	COLUMN 3	
11.	QLNRCA	931268	iregnd	11._____
12.	NRMOTC	127546	egftbn	12._____
13.	RCTALM	265837	gndbrt	13._____
14.	TAMLON	578341	bdtrfe	14._____
15.	ANTORM	815427	debigt	15._____
16.	MRALON	728341	tgdrfe	16._____
17.	CTNQRO	657924	ndeigf	17._____
18.	QMROTA	972458	itgfbd	18._____
19.	RQMCOL	297463	gitnfr	19._____
20.	NOMRTQ	147259	eftgbi	20._____

Questions 21-25.

DIRECTIONS: Questions 21 through 25 are to be answered SOLELY on the basis of the following passage.

The city may issue its own bonds or it may purchase bonds as an investment. Bonds may be issued in various denominations, and the face value of the bond is its par value. Before purchasing a bond, the investor desires to know the rate of income that the investment may yield in computing the yield on a bond, it is assumed that the investor will keep the bond until the date of maturity, except for callable bonds which are not considered in this passage. To compute exact yield is a complicated mathematical problem, and scientifically prepared tables are generally used to avoid such computation. However, the approximate yield can be computed much more easily. In computing approximate yield, the accrued interest on the date of purchase should be ignored because the buyer who pays accrued interest to the seller receives it again at the next interest date. Bonds bought at a premium (which cost more) yield a lower rate of income than the same bonds bought at par (face value), and bounds bought at a discount (which cost less) yield a higher rate of income than the same bonds bought at par.

21. An investor bought a $10,000 city bond paying 6% interest. Which of the following purchase prices would indicate that the bond was bought at a premium?   21._____
    A. $9,000   B. $9,400   C. $10,000   D. $10,600

22. During 2016, a particular $10,000 bond paying 7 ½% sold at fluctuating prices. Which of the following prices would indicate that the bond was bought at a discount?   22._____
    A. $9,800   B. $10,000   C. $10,200   D. $10,750

23. A certain group of bonds was sold in denominations of $5,000, $10,000, $20,000, and $50,000.
In the following list of four purchase prices, which one is MOST likely to represent a bond sold at par value?
    A. $10,500   B. $20,000   C. $22,000   D. $49,000

24. When computing the approximate yield on a bond, it is DESIRABLE to
    A. assume the bond was purchased at par
    B. consult scientifically prepared tables
    C. ignore accrued interest on the date of purchase
    D. wait until the bond reaches maturity

25. Which of the following is MOST likely to be an exception to the information provided in the above passage?
    Bonds
    A. purchased at a premium
    B. sold at par
    C. sold before maturity
    D. which are callable

KEY (CORRECT ANSWERS)

1.	B		11.	D
2.	C		12.	C
3.	D		13.	B
4.	A		14.	A
5.	D		15.	B
6.	D		16.	D
7.	A		17.	C
8.	D		18.	D
9.	D		19.	A
10.	C		20.	D

21.	D
22.	A
23.	B
24.	C
25.	D

TEST 3

DIRECTIONS: Each question or incomplete statement is followed by several suggested answers or completions. Select the one that BEST answers the question or completes the statement. *PRINT THE LETTER OF THE CORRECT ANSWER IN THE SPACE AT THE RIGHT.*

Questions 1-6.

DIRECTIONS: Questions 1 through 6 consist of computations of addition, subtraction, multiplication, and division. For each question, do the computation indicated, and choose the correct answer from the four choices given.

1. ADD: 8936
   7821
   8953
   4297
   9785
   6579

   A. 45371   B. 45381   C. 46371   D. 46381

   1.____

2. SUBTRACT: 95,432
   67,596

   A. 27,836   B. 27,846   C. 27,936   D. 27,946

   2.____

3. MULTIPLY: 987
   867

   A. 854609   B. 854729   C. 855709   D. 855729

   3.____

4. DIVIDE: 59)321439.0

   A. 5438.1   B. 5447.1   C. 5448.1   D. 5457.1

   4.____

5. DIVIDE: .057)721

   A. 12,648.0   B. 12,648.1   C. 12,649.0   D. 12,649.1

   5.____

6. ADD: 1/2 + 5/7
   A. 1 3/14   B. 1 2/7   C. 1 5/14   D. 1 3/7

   6.____

7. If the total number of employees in one city agency increased from 1,927 to 2,006 during a certain year, the percentage increase in the number of employees for that year is MOST NEARLY
   A. 4%   B. 5%   C. 6%   D. 7%

   7.____

8. During a single fiscal year, which totaled 248 workdays, one account clerk verified 1,488 purchase vouchers.
Assuming a normal work week of five days, what is the average number of vouchers verified by the account clerk in a one-week period during this fiscal year?
A. 25 B. 30 C. 35 D. 40

9. If the city department of purchase bought 190 computers for $793.50 each and 208 computers for $839.90 each, the TOTAL price paid for these computers is
A. $315,813.00 B. $325,464.20
C. $334,279.20 D. $335,863.00

Questions 10-14.

DIRECTIONS: Questions 10 through 14 are to be answered SOLELY on the basis of the information given in the following paragraph.

Since discounts are in common use in the commercial world and apply to purchases made by government agencies as well as business firms, it is essential that individuals in both public and private employment who prepare bills, check invoices, prepare payment vouchers, or write checks to pay bills have an understanding of the terms used. These include cash or time discount, trade discount, and disconnect series. A cash or time discount offers a reduction in price to the buyer for the prompt payment of the bill and is usually expressed as a percentage with a time requirement, stated in days, within which the bill must be paid in order to earn the discount. An example would be 3/10, meaning a 3% discount may be applied to the bill if the payment is forwarded to the vendor within ten days. On an invoice, the cash discount terms are usually followed by the net terms, which is the time in days allowed for ordinary payment of the bill. Thus, 3/10, Net 30 means that full payment is expected in thirty days if the cash discount of 3% is not taken for having paid the bill within ten days. When the expression Terms Net Cash is listed on a bill, it means that no deduction for early payment is allowed. A trade discount is normally applied to list prices by a manufacturer to show the actual price to retailers so that they may know their cost and determine markups that will allow them to operate competitively and at a profit. A trade discount is applied by the seller to the list price and is independent of a cash or time discount. Discounts may also be used by manufacturers to adjust prices charged to retailers without changing list prices. This is usually done by series discounting and is expressed as a series of percentages. To compute a series discount, such as 40%, 20%, 10%, first apply the 40% discount to the list price, then apply the 20% discount to the remainder, and finally apply the 10% discount to the second remainder.

10. According to the above passage, trade discounts are
A. applied by the buyer B. independent of cash discounts
C. restricted to cash sales D. used to secure rapid payment of bills

11. According to the above passage, if the sales terms 5/10, Net 60 appear on a bill in the amount of $100 dated December 5, 2016 and the buyer submits his payment on December 15, 2016, his PROPER payment should be
A. $60 B. $90 C. $95 D. $100

12. According to the above passage, if a manufacturer gives a trade discount of 40% for an item with a list price of $250 and the terms are Net Cash, the price a retail merchant is required to pay for this item is
    A. $250   B. $210   C. $150   D. $100

13. According to the above passage, a series discount of 25%, 20%, 10% applied to a list price of $200 results in an ACTUAL price to the buyer of
    A. $88   B. $90   C. $108   D. $110

14. According to the above passage, if a manufacturer gives a trade discount of 50% and the terms are 6/10, Net 30, the cost to a retail merchant of an item with a list price of $500 and for which he takes the time discount is
    A. $220   B. $235   C. $240   D. $250

Questions 15-22.

DIRECTIONS: Questions 15 through 22 each show in Column I the information written on five cards (lettered j, k, l, m, n) which have to be filed. You are to choose the option (lettered A, B, C, or D) in Column II which BEST represents the proper order of filing according to the information, rules, and sample question given below.

A file card record is kept of the work assignments for all the employees in a certain bureau. On each card is the employee's name, the date of work assignment, and the work assignment code number. The cards are to be filed according to the following rules:

FIRST: File in alphabetical order according to employee's name.

SECOND: When two or more cards have the same employee's name, file according to the assignment date, beginning with the earliest date.

THIRD: When two or more cards have the same employee's name and the same date, file according to the work assignment number beginning with the lowest number.

Column II shows the cards arranged in four different orders. Pick the option (A, B, C, or D) in Column II which shows the correct arrangement of the cards according to th above filing rules.

SAMPLE QUESTION

Column I
j. Cluney 4/8/02 (486503)
k. Roster 5/10/01 (246611)
l. Altool 10/15/02 (711433)
m. Cluney 12/18/02 (527610)
n. Cluney 4/8/02 (486500)

Column II
A. k, l, m, j, n
B. k, n, j, l, m
C. l, k, j, m, n
D. l, n, j, m, k

4 (#3)

The correct way to file the cards is:
- l. Altool 10/15/02 (71143)
- n. Cluney 4/8/02 (486500)
- j. Cluney 4/8/02 (486503)
- m. Cluney 12/18/02 (527610)
- k. Roster 5/10/01 (246611)

The correct filing order is shown by the letters l, n, j, m, k. The answer to the sample question is the letter D, which appears in front of the letters l, n, j, m, k in Column II.

COLUMN I   COLUMN II

15. j. Smith 3/19/03 (662118)   A. j, m, l, n, k   15.____
     k. Turner 4/16/99 (481349)   B. j, l, n, m, k
     l. Terman 3/20/02 (210229)   C. k, n, m, l, j
     m. Smyth 3/20/02 (481359)   D. j, n, k, l, m
     n. Terry 5/11/01 (672128)

16. j. Ross 5/29/02 (396118)   A. l, m, k, n, j   16.____
     k. Rosner 5/29/02 (439281)   B. m, l, k, n, j
     l. Rose 7/19/02 (723456)   C. l, m, k, j, n
     m. Rosen 5/29/03 (829692)   D. m, l, j, n, k
     n. Ross 5/29/02 (399118)

17. j. Sherd 10/12/99 (552368)   A. n, m, k, j, l   17.____
     k. Snyder 11/12/99 (539286)   B. j, m, l, k, n
     l. Shindler 10/13/98 (426798)   C. m, k, n, j. l
     m. Scherld 10/12/99 (552386)   D. m, n, j, l, k
     n. Schneider 11/12/99 (798213)

18. j. Carter 1/16/02 (489636)   A. k, n, j, l, m   18.____
     k. Carson 2/16/01 (392671)   B. n, k, m, l, j
     l. Carter 1/16/01 (486936)   C. n, k, l, j, m
     m. Carton 3/15/00 (489639)   D. k, n, l, j, m
     n. Carson 2/16/01 (392617)

19. j. Thomas 3/18/99 (763182)   A. m, l, j, k, n   19.____
     k. Tompkins 3/19/00 (928439)   B. j, m, l, k, n
     l. Thomson 3/21/00 (763812)   C. j, l, n, m, k
     m. Thompson 3/18/99 (924893)   D. l, m, j, n, k
     n. Tompson 3/19/99 (928793)

20. j. Breit 8/10/03 (345612)   A. m, j, n, k, l   20.____
     k. Briet 5/21/00 (837543)   B. n, m, j, k, l
     l. Bright 9/18/99 (931827)   C. m, j, k, l, n
     m. Breit 3/7/98 (553984)   D. j, m, k, l, n
     n. Brent 6/14/04 (682731)

COLUMN I	COLUMN II

21.	j.	Roberts 10/19/02 (581932)	A.	n, k, l, m, j	21._____
	k.	Rogers 8/9/00 (638763)	B.	n, k, l, j, m
	l.	Rogers 7/15/97 (105689)	C.	k, n, l, m, j
	m.	Robin 3/8/92 (287915)	D.	j, m, k, n, l
	n.	Rogers 4/2/04 (736921)

22.	j.	Hebert 4/28/02 (719468)	A.	n, k, j, m, l	22._____
	k.	Herbert 5/8/01 (938432)	B.	j, l, n, k, m
	l.	Helbert 9/23/04 (832912)	C.	l, j, k, n, m
	m.	Herbst 7/10/03 (648599)	D.	l, j, n, k, m
	n.	Herbert 5/8/01 (487627)

23.	In order to pay its employees, the Convex Company obtained bills and coins	23._____
	in the following denominations:

Denomination	$20	$10	$5	$1	$.50	$.25	$.10	$.05	$.01
Number	317	122	38	73	69	47	39	25	36

   What was the TOTAL amount of cash obtained?
   A. $7,874.76	B. $7,878.00	C. $7,889.25	D. $7,924.35

24.	H. Partridge receives a weekly gross salary (before deductions) of $596.25.	24._____
	Through weekly payroll deductions of $19.77, he is paying back a load he took
	from his pension fund.
	If other fixed weekly deductions amount to $184.14, how much pay would Mr.
	Partridge take home over a period of 33 weeks?
	   A. $11,446.92	B. $12,375.69	C. $12,947.22	D. $19,676.25

25.	Mr. Robertson is a city employee enrolled in a city retirement system. He has	25._____
	taken out a loan from the retirement fund and is paying it back at the rate of
	$14.90 every two weeks.
	In eighteen weeks, how much money will he have paid back on the loan?
	   A. $268.20	B. $152.80	C. $124.10	D. $67.05

26.	In 2015, the Iridor Book Company had the following expenses: rent, $6,500;	26._____
	overhead, $52,585; inventory, $35,700; and miscellaneous, $1,275.
	If all of these expenses went up 18% in 2016, what would they TOTAL in 2016?
	   A. $17,290.80	B. $78,768.20	C. $96,060.00	D. $113,350.80

27.	Ms. Ranier had a gross salary of $355.36, paid once every week.	27._____
	If the deductions from each paycheck are $62.72, $25.13, $6.29, and $1,27, how
	much money would Ms. Ranier take home in four weeks?
	   A. $1,039.80	B. $1,421.44	C. $2,079.60	D. $2,842.88

28. Mr. Martin had a net income of $19,100 for the year. 28.____
If he spent 34% on rent and household expenses, 3% on house furnishings, 25% on clothes, and 36% on food, how much was left for savings and other expenses?
   A. $196.00   B. $382.00   C. $649.40   D. $1,960.00

29. Mr. Elsberg can pay back a loan of $1,800 from the city employees' retirement 29.____
system if he pays back $36.69 every two weeks for two full years.
At the end of the two years, how much more than the original $1,800 he borrowed will Mr. Elsberg have paid back?
   A. $53.94   B. $107.88   C. $190.79   D. $214.76

30. Mrs. Nusbaum is a city employee, receiving a gross salary (salary before 30.____
deductions) of $31,200. Every two weeks, the following deductions are taken out of her salary: Federal Income Tax, $243.96; FICA, $66.39; State Tax, $44.58; City Tax, $20.91; Health Insurance, $4.71.
If Mrs. Nusbaum's salary and deductions remained the same for a full calendar year, what would her NET salary (gross salary less deductions) be in that year?
   A. $9,894.30   B. $21,305.70   C. $28,118.25   D. $30,819.45

KEY (CORRECT ANSWERS)

1.	C	11.	C	21.	D
2.	A	12.	C	22.	B
3.	D	13.	C	33.	A
4.	C	14.	B	24.	C
5.	D	15.	A	25.	C
6.	A	16.	C	26.	D
7.	A	17.	D	27.	A
8.	B	18.	C	28.	B
9.	B	19.	B	29.	B
10.	B	20.	A	30.	B

EXAMINATION SECTION
TEST 1

DIRECTIONS: Each question or incomplete statement is followed by several suggested answers or completions. Select the one that BEST answers the question or completes the statement. *PRINT THE LETTER OF THE CORRECT ANSWER IN THE SPACE AT THE RIGHT.*

Questions 1-7.

DIRECTIONS: Questions 1 through 7 are to be answered on the basis of the following income statement.

Laura Lee's Bridal Shop
Income Statement
For the Year Ended December 31, 2018

Revenue:		
New & Used Bridal Gowns & Accessories		$55,000
Expenses:		
Advertisement Expense	$ 2,000	
Salaries Expense	12,000	
Dry cleaning & Alterations	10,000	
Utilities	1,500	
Total Expenses		25,500
Net Income		$29,500

1. What is the period of time covered by this income statement?   1.____

    A. January-December 2017
    B. December 2018
    C. January 2017-December 2018
    D. January-December 2018

2. What is the source of the revenue?   2.____

    A. New and used bridal gowns, advertisements, salaries, dry cleaning, and utilities
    B. Advertisements, salaries, dry cleaning, alterations, and utilities
    C. New and used bridal gowns and accessories
    D. Net income

3. What is the total revenue?   3.____

    A. $25,500   B. $55,000   C. $29,500   D. $79,500

4. Which of the following are expenses?   4.____

    A. Salaries
    B. New and used bridal gowns and accessories
    C. Revenue
    D. New and used bridal gowns, advertisements, and dry cleaning

5. What are the total expenses?   5.____

    A. $55,000   B. $29,500   C. $79,500   D. $25,500

6. There is a resulting net income because

   A. total revenue and total expenses are combined
   B. net income is greater than total revenue
   C. the total revenue is greater than total expenses
   D. the total revenue is less than total expenses

7. Is this statement an interim statement?

   A. Yes, because it covers an entire accounting period
   B. No, because it covers an entire accounting period
   C. Yes, because it covers a period of less than a year
   D. No, because it covers a period of more than a year

8. What is the name of the accounting report that may show either a net profit or a net loss for an accounting period?

   A. Income statement
   B. Balance sheet
   C. Statement of capital
   D. Classified balance sheet

9. What are the two main parts of the body of the income statement?

   A. Cash and Capital
   B. Revenue and Expenses
   C. Liabilities and Capital
   D. Assets and Notes Payable

10. If total revenue exceeds total expenses for an accounting period, what is the difference called?

    A. Gross income
    B. Total liabilities
    C. Total assets
    D. Net income

11. In the body of a balance sheet, what are the three sections called?

    A. Assets and liabilities
    B. Cash, liabilities, and revenue
    C. Assets, liabilities, and capital
    D. Revenue, assets, and capital

12. What business record shows the results of the proprietor's borrowing assets from the business, usually in anticipation of profits?

    A. Proprietor's withdrawals
    B. Accounts payable
    C. Liabilities and Capital
    D. Total liabilities

Questions 13-24.

DIRECTIONS: For each transaction given for Mona's Magic Moments Hair Salon in Questions 13 through 24, identify which journal the transaction should be recorded in.

13. April 1: Mona, the owner, paid the month's rent - $600.00; check no. 356.

    A. General
    B. Cash disbursements
    C. Purchases
    D. Sales

14. April 6: the salon purchased $300.00 worth of styling products on account from Pomme de Terre Company.   14._____

    A. Cash disbursements   B. General
    C. Sales   D. Purchases

15. April 8: sold $100.00 worth of hair products on account to Mrs. Angela Bray.   15._____

    A. Sales   B. Purchases
    C. Cash disbursements   D. General

16. April 11: the owner, Mona Ramen, withdrew $80.00 of styling products for personal use.   16._____

    A. Sales   B. Cash receipts
    C. General   D. Cash disbursements

17. April 13: paid Pomme de Terre Company $300.00 on account; check 357.   17._____

    A. Purchases   B. Cash disbursements
    C. Cash receipts   D. General

18. April 15: cash sales to date were $4,607.00.   18._____

    A. Cash disbursements   B. Purchases
    C. Sales   D. General

19. April 17: issued credit slip #17 to Mrs. Angela Bray for $25.00 for merchandise returned.   19._____

    A. Cash disbursements   B. Cash receipts
    C. Sales   D. General

20. April 19: paid electric bill for $250.00; check no. 358.   20._____

    A. Cash disbursements   B. Purchases
    C. General   D. Cash receipts

21. April 21: received $75.00 from Mrs. Angela Bray for balance due on account.   21._____

    A. Sales   B. Cash disbursements
    C. Cash receipts   D. Purchases

22. April 23: sold $88.00 of hair products on account to Ms. Tania Alioto.   22._____

    A. Purchases   B. Sales
    C. Cash disbursements   D. Cash receipts

23. April 27: purchased $500.00 of equipment from Salon Stylings Merchandisers on account.   23._____

    A. Cash disbursements   B. Sales
    C. General   D. Purchases

24. April 30: cash sales to date were $5023.00.   24._____

    A. Purchases   B. Sales
    C. Cash receipts   D. General

Questions 25-30.

DIRECTIONS: Questions 25 through 30 are to be answered on the basis of the following ledger for a barbecue take-out restaurant owned and operated by Ruby Joiner.

Cash		Accounts Receivable		Delivery Equipment	
450	150	360	170	5,000	
212	125	250	100	4,000	
328	440	165	120	3,000	
172	125	100	60		
250	70				
275	150				
325	50				

Supplies		Ruby Joiner, Capital		Accounts Payable	
40			8,200	10	600
65			2,000	15	300
30			2,097		200
25					

Ruby Joiner, Drawing		Advertising Expense		Delivery Income	
225		40			400
175		45			350
200					250
					100

Trucking Expense		Telephone Expense	
100		80	
50		40	
		20	

25. What is the balance on the Cash account shown above?

   A. 2,012.00   B. 1,110.00   C. 3,122.00   D. 902.00

26. What is the balance on the Accounts receivable account shown above?

   A. 425.00   B. 875.00   C. 450.00   D. 1315.00

27. What is the balance on the Accounts payable account shown above?

   A. 1100.00   B. 1075.00   C. 25.00   D. 1125.00

28. Which of the above accounts has a balance of 1100.00?

   A. Accounts payable
   B. Delivery Income
   C. Cash
   D. Delivery equipment

29. Which of the above accounts has a balance of 12,000.00?

   A. Ruby Joiner, Capital
   B. Cash and Accounts receivable combined
   C. Delivery equipment
   D. None of the accounts

30. If you made a balance sheet out of the information listed above, Ruby Joiner's total assets would be

   A. 14,472.00   B. 12,297.00   C. 13,392.00   D. 13,487.00

Questions 31-34.

DIRECTIONS: Questions 31 through 34 are to be answered on the basis of the following information, to be included on a checking deposit ticket.

Five $20 bills; 11 $10 bills; 6 $5 bills; 47 $1 bills; 200 half dollars; 120 quarters; 112 dimes; 320 nickels; 67 pennies. Second National Bank (73-124) check of 152.34; Bank of the Midwest (13-298) check of 68.37; Great National Bank (32-165) check of 185.06.

31. What is the TOTAL currency for this deposit?   31._____
    A. $387   B. $287   C. $444.87   D. $157.87

32. What is the TOTAL coin for this deposit?   32._____
    A. $387   B. $287   C. $444.87   D. $157.87

33. What is the check total for this deposit?   33._____
    A. $692.77   B. $406   C. $405.77   D. $850.64

34. What is the TOTAL deposit?   34._____
    A. $444.87   B. $692.77   C. $851   D. $850.64

Questions 35-37.

DIRECTIONS: Questions 35 through 37 are to be answered on the basis of the following petty cash journal.

Date	Receipt No.	To Whom Paid	For What	Acct.#	Amount
10/2	1	Anna Jones - Mail	Postage	548	13.50
10/2	2	Jim Collins	Messenger	525	5.75
10/4	3	Anna Jones - Mail	Postage	548	13.50
10/5	4	Lucky Stores	Coffee	515	7.34
10/6	5	Tom Allen	Lunch w/customer	525	11.38

35. What is the TOTAL disbursement from this fund for the time period 10/1 through 10/6?   35._____
    A. $51.47   B. $40.09   C. $61.47   D. $26.59

36. How much money was disbursed to Account #548 during the time period 10/1-10/16?   36._____
    A. $51.47   B. $26   C. $27   D. $34.34

37. If the fund began the month with a total of $100.00, what amount was left in the fund at the end of business on 10/5?   37._____
    A. $48.53   B. $59.91   C. $51.47   D. $40.09

Questions 38-40.

DIRECTIONS: Questions 38 through 40 are to be answered on the basis of the following information.

A promissory note dated December 1, 2018, bearing interest at a rate of 12% and due in 90 days, is sent to a creditor. The face value of the note is $900.

38. What is the due date of the promissory note? 38.____

   A. January 15, 2019   B. March 1, 2019
   C. February 1, 2019   D. December 31, 2018

39. What is the TOTAL interest that will be earned on the note? 39.____

   A. $27   B. $270   C. $108   D. $10.80

40. What interest will be earned on the note for the old accounting period (December 1-31)? 40.____

   A. $90   B. $36   C. $9   D. $3.60

KEY (CORRECT ANSWERS)

1. D	11. C	21. C	31. B
2. C	12. A	22. B	32. D
3. B	13. B	23. D	33. C
4. A	14. D	24. B	34. D
5. D	15. A	25. D	35. A
6. C	16. C	26. A	36. C
7. B	17. B	27. B	37. B
8. A	18. C	28. B	38. B
9. B	19. D	29. C	39. A
10. D	20. A	30. D	40. C

TEST 2

DIRECTIONS: Each question or incomplete statement is followed by several suggested answers or completions. Select the one that BEST answers the question or completes the statement. *PRINT THE LETTER OF THE CORRECT ANSWER IN THE SPACE AT THE RIGHT.*

Questions 1-4.

DIRECTIONS: Questions 1 through 4 are to be answered on the basis of the following information, to be included in a deposit slip.

    14 twenty dollar bills   63 quarters
    52 ten dollar bills   22 dimes
    12 five dollar bills   44 nickels
    43 one dollar bills   70 pennies

Checks: $236.34 and $129.72

1. What is the TOTAL amount of currency for this deposit?   1._____
     A. $923.85   B. $1269.06   C. $903.00   D. $1299.91

2. What is the TOTAL amount of coin for this deposit?   2._____
     A. $20.85   B. $923.85   C. $903.00   D. $1299.91

3. What is the TOTAL amount of check for this deposit?   3._____
     A. $20.85   B. $366.06   C. $1299.91   D. $903.00

4. What is the TOTAL deposit for this slip?   4._____
     A. $1269.06   B. $903.00   C. $923.85   D. $1289.91

Questions 5-7.

DIRECTIONS: Questions 5 through 7 are to be answered on the basis of the following information.

Angela Martinez's last check stub balance was $675.50. Her bank statement balance dated April 30 was $652.00. A $250 deposit was in transit on that date. Outstanding checks were as follows: No. 127, $65.00; No. 129, $203.50; No. 130, $50.00. The bank service charge for the month was $5.00.

5. What was Angela Martinez's available checkbook balance on April 30?   5._____
     A. $652.00   B. $338.50   C. $583.50   D. $675.50

6. In order to reconcile her checkbook balance with her bank statement balance, what must Angela Martinez do?   6._____

     A. Add her checkbook balance to the balance on her bank statement
     B. Subtract her checkbook balance from the balance on her bank statement

C. Ignore her checkbook balance and adopt the balance on her bank statement
D. Adjust the checkbook balance by adding deposits and debiting outstanding checks and charges

7. The check stub balance referred to in the problem refers to the 7.____

   A. last check Angela Martinez recorded in her checkbook
   B. amount of money left in Angela Martinez's account according to her own calculations based on the checks, charges, and deposits she has written and recorded
   C. amount of money left in Angela Martinez's account according to the bank's calculations based on the checks, charges, and deposits posted to her account
   D. number of checks left in her checkbook

Questions 8-9.

DIRECTIONS: Questions 8 and 9 are to be answered on the basis of the following information.

Tu Nguyen, an interior designer, received his June bank statement on July 2. The balance was $622.66. His last check stub balance was $700. On comparing the two, he noticed that a deposit of $275 made on June 30 was not included on the statement; also, a bank service charge of $4 was deducted. Outstanding checks were as follows: No. 331, $97.50; No. 332, $207; No. 335, $25.40; and No. 336, $68.97.

8. What is Nguyen's CORRECT available bank balance? 8.____

   A. $494.79   B. $897.66   C. $700.00   D. $219.79

9. The bank statement balance referred to in the problem refers to the 9.____

   A. last check Tu Nguyen recorded in his checkbook
   B. last check presented for payment to Tu Nguyen's account
   C. amount of money left in Tu Nguyen's account according to the bank's calculations based on the checks, charges, and deposits posted to his account
   D. amount of money left in Tu Nguyen's account based on his own calculations of the checks, charges, and deposits he has written and recorded

10. What of the following endorsements would be an example of a simple Endorsement in Blank? 10.____

    A. Pay to the Order of Joanie Anderson
    B. Joanie Anderson
    C. For deposit only; Acct. No. 12345; Joanie Anderson
    D. Without Recourse; Joanie Anderson

11. Which of the following endorsements would limit the further purpose or use of the endorsed check? 11.____

    A. Pay to the Order of Joanie Anderson
    B. Joanie Anderson
    C. For deposit only; Acct. No. 12345; Joanie Anderson,
    D. Without Recourse; Joanie Anderson

12. Which of the following endorsements would protect the endorser from legal responsibility for payment, should the drawer have insufficient funds to honor his/her own check?   12._____

    A. Pay to the Order of Joanie Anderson
    B. Joanie Anderson
    C. For deposit only; Acct. No. 12345; Joanie Anderson
    D. Without Recourse; Joanie Anderson

Questions 13-24.

DIRECTIONS: Questions 13 - 24 are to be answered on the basis of the following ledger accounts for Wheelsmith Organic Farms.

Wheelsmith Organic Farms
Ledger Accounts

Cash	Accounts Payable	Service Supplies
Jan. 1 4,000	Jan. 1 2,000	Jan. 1 2,000

Shelley Wheelsmith, Capital	Machinery
Jan. 1 11,000	Jan. 1 7,000

13. Transaction #1: On January 5, Shelley Wheelsmith, the proprietor, received cash amounting to $5,000 as a result of returning machinery that had recently been purchased. What account(s) should this transaction be posted to?   13._____

    A. Cash
    B. Cash and Machinery
    C. Machinery
    D. Cash, Machinery, and Service Supplies

14. Transaction #2: On January 8, Shelley Wheelsmith, the proprietor, sent out a check for $600 in partial payment of the accounts payable.   14._____
    What account(s) should this transaction be posted to?

    A. Accounts Payable
    B. Accounts Payable and Cash
    C. Accounts Payable and Capital
    D. Cash

15. Transaction #3: On January 14, Shelley Wheelsmith, proprietor, made an additional investment in the business by contributing machinery valued at $1,500.   15._____
    What account(s) should this transaction be posted to?

    A. Machinery   B. Machinery and Capital
    C. Capital   D. Machinery and Cash

16. Transaction #4: On January 26, Shelley Wheelsmith, proprietor, purchased additional service supplies for $200. She agreed to pay the obligation in 30 days. What account(s) should this transaction be posted to?   16._____

A. Accounts Payable and Liabilities
B. Service supplies
C. Accounts Payable
D. Accounts Payable and Service supplies

17. Transaction #5: On January 31, Shelley Wheelsmith, proprietor, purchased service supplies paying cash of $50. What account(s) should this transaction be posted to?   17.____

A. Service supplies
B. Service supplies and Accounts Payable
C. Cash and Service supplies
D. Cash

18. What is the balance in the Cash account after all of these transactions are posted?   18.____

A. $9,000   B. $1,000   C. $5,000   D. $8,350

19. What is the balance in the Machinery account after all of these transactions are posted?   19.____

A. $7,000   B. $5,000   C. $3,500   D. $13,500

20. What is the balance in the Accounts Payable account after all of these transactions are posted?   20.____

A. $800   B. $600   C. $2,600   D. $1,600

21. What is the balance in the Capital account after all of these transactions are posted?   21.____

A. $12,500   B. $800   C. $11,600   D. $10,400

22. What is the balance in the Service supplies account after all of these transactions are posted?   22.____

A. $2,000   B. $2,250   C. $750   D. $2,200

23. What are the total assets of Wheelsmith Organic Farms after these transactions have been posted?   23.____

A. $10,600   B. $11,850   C. $14,100   D. $10,750

24. What are the total liabilities and capital for Wheelsmith Organic Farms after these transactions have been posted?   24.____

A. $14,100   B. $12,500   C. $11,850   D. $10,600

Questions 25-28.

DIRECTIONS: Questions 25 through 28 are to be answered on the basis of the following information.

At the end of an accounting period, Andy's Framing Gallery recorded the following information: Sales, $125,225; Merchandise Inventory, December 31, $95,325; Purchases Returns and Allowances, $3,500; Merchandise Inventory, January 1, $98,725; Freight on Purchases, $2,500; Purchases, $120,000.

25. What are the net purchases for Andy's Framing Gallery during the accounting period? 25.____
    A. $120,000   B. $119,000   C. $3,500   D. $122,500

26. What is the cost of goods available for sale? 26.____
    A. $119,000   B. $98,725   C. $95,325   D. $217,725

27. What is the total cost of goods sold for this accounting period? 27.____
    A. $217,725   B. $95,325   C. $122,400   D. $125,225

28. What is the gross profit on sales for this accounting period? 28.____
    A. $2825   B. $2500   C. $125,225   D. $122,400

Questions 29-40.

DIRECTIONS: Questions 29 through 40 are to be answered on the basis of the following information.

The Joie de Vivre Co. received the promissory notes listed below during the last quarter of its calendar year:

	Date	Face Amount	Terms	Interest Rate	Date Discounted	Discount Rate
(1)	10/8	$3,600	30 days	-	10/18	9%
(2)	9/22	$8,000	60 days	6%	10/1	7%
(3)	11/15	$3,000	90 days	7%	11/20	8%

29. What is the due date for the first note? 29.____
    A. 12/31   B. 11/7   C. 12/7   D. 10/31

30. What interest will be due when the first note matures? 30.____
    A. $3   B. $3,600   C. $30   D. $0

31. What is the maturity value of the first note? 31.____
    A. $3,600   B. $3,630   C. $0   D. $3,603

32. What is the discount period for the first note? 32.____
    A. One fiscal year   B. 10 days
    C. 20 days   D. One month

33. What is the due date for the second note? 33.____
    A. 12/21   B. 11/21   C. 10/21   D. 1/21

34. What interest will be due when the second note matures? 34.____
    A. $60   B. $800.00   C. $8.00   D. $80.00

35. What is the maturity value of the second note? 35.____
    A. $8,000   B. $8,080   C. $8,800   D. $8,008

6 (#2)

36. What is the discount period for the second note? 36._____
    A. 51 days B. 10 days C. 360 days D. 60 days

37. What is the due date for the third note? 37._____
    A. 1/14 B. 12/15 C. 12/31 D. 2/13

38. What interest will be due when the third note matures? 38._____
    A. $5.25 B. $52.50 C. $525 D. $90

39. What is the maturity value of the third note? 39._____
    A. $3525 B. $3005.25 C. $3052.50 D. $3090

40. What is the discount period for the third note? 40._____
    A. 60 days B. 85 days C. 5 days D. 90 days

KEY (CORRECT ANSWERS)

1.	C	11.	C	21.	A	31.	A
2.	A	12.	D	22.	B	32.	C
3.	B	13.	B	23.	C	33.	B
4.	D	14.	B	24.	A	34.	D
5.	C	15.	B	25.	B	35.	B
6.	D	16.	D	26.	D	36.	A
7.	B	17.	C	27.	C	37.	D
8.	A	18.	D	28.	A	38.	B
9.	C	19.	C	29.	B	39.	C
10.	B	20.	D	30.	D	40.	B

TEST 3

DIRECTIONS: Each question or incomplete statement is followed by several suggested answers or completions. Select the one that BEST answers the question or completes the statement. *PRINT THE LETTER OF THE CORRECT ANSWER IN THE SPACE AT THE RIGHT.*

Questions 1-8.

DIRECTIONS: Questions 1 through 8 are to be answered on the basis of the following Balance Sheet.

Laura Lee's Bridal Shop
Balance Sheet
December 31, 2018

Assets
Cash	$14,000	
Accounts Receivable	3,000	
Bridal Accessories	10,000	
Gowns and Other Inventory	30,000	
Total Assets		$57,000

Liabilities and Capital
Accounts Payable	$ 4,000	
Notes Payable	28,000	
Total Liabilities		$32,000
Laura Lee, Capital		25,000
Total Liabilities and Capital		$57,000

1. When was the balance sheet prepared?

   A. January 2019
   B. December 31, 2018
   C. After the close of the 2018 fiscal year
   D. December 1, 2018

2. How does the date on this balance sheet differ from the date on the statement of capital or income statement?

   A. It doesn't differ. The dates for each statement signify the same time period.
   B. The date on a balance sheet represents the period during which any changes indicated on the statement took place, whereas the other financial statements represent the moment in time when the statement was prepared.
   C. The date on a balance sheet represents the moment in time when the statement was prepared, whereas the other financial statements represent the period during which any changes indicated on the statement took place.
   D. The date on a balance sheet indicates an entire year, whereas the dates on the other statements indicate a single month.

3. Can Laura Lee purchase more bridal gowns for the business paying cash of $16,000?

   A. *No*, because the business has only $14,000 cash available
   B. *Yes*, because the business has $57,000 cash available
   C. *Yes*, because the business has $57,000 available in assets
   D. *No*, because the business has $57,000 in liabilities

1.____

2.____

3.____

2 (#3)

4. What is the owner's equity of Laura Lee's Bridal Shop?
   Since total equity consists of total _____, total equity is _____.

   A. assets minus total liabilities and proprietor's capital; $0
   B. assets minus total liabilities; $25,000
   C. assets; $57,000
   D. liabilities and proprietor's capital; $57,000

5. What is the TOTAL amount of Laura Lee's claim against the total assets of the business?

   A. $57,000   B. $25,000   C. $0   D. $39,000

6. What is the amount of the creditors' claims against the assets of the business?

   A. $4,000   B. $57,000   C. $32,000   D. $28,000

7. What is the net income for the period?

   A. $57,000
   B. $0
   C. $25,000
   D. This information cannot be obtained from the balance sheet

8. What was the value of Laura Lee's ownership in this business on January 1, 2004?

   A. $25,000
   B. $57,000
   C. $14,000
   D. This information cannot be obtained from the balance sheet

Questions 9-21.

DIRECTIONS: Each of the transactions described in Questions 9 through 21 occurred within an accounting period. For each question, indicate which of the four journals the transaction would be recorded in.

9. Sale of goods on account

   A. Cash receipts   B. Cash payments
   C. General   D. Sales

10. Cash payment of a promissory note

    A. Cash payments   B. Cash receipts
    C. Sales   D. General

11. Received a credit memo from a creditor

    A. Purchases   B. General
    C. Sales   D. Cash payments

12. Sale of merchandise for cash

    A. Purchases   B. General
    C. Cash receipts   D. Cash payments

13. Received a check from a customer in partial payment of an oral agreement   13.____

    A. Purchases   B. Sales
    C. General   D. Cash receipts

14. Issued a credit memo to a customer   14.____

    A. Purchases   B. General
    C. Cash payments   D. Sales

15. Received a promissory note in place of an oral agreement from a customer   15.____

    A. General   B. Cash payments
    C. Cash receipts   D. Sales

16. Paid monthly rent   16.____

    A. General   B. Purchases
    C. Cash payments   D. Cash receipts

17. Sale of a service on credit   17.____

    A. Cash receipts   B. General
    C. Purchases   D. Sales

18. Purchase of office furniture on credit   18.____

    A. General   B. Purchases
    C. Cash payments   D. Cash receipts

19. Purchased merchandise for cash   19.____

    A. Cash payments   B. Cash receipts
    C. Sales   D. General

20. Cash refund to a customer   20.____

    A. Cash receipts   B. Sales
    C. General   D. Cash payments

21. Purchases made on credit   21.____

    A. Purchases   B. Sales
    C. Cash receipts   D. General

Questions 22-26.

DIRECTIONS: Questions 22 through 26 are to be answered on the basis of the following inventory, purchased by International Soap and Candle Traders, Inc.

700 units at $4.50, 320 units at $3.75, 550 units at $2.75, and 475 units at $1.90

22. Calculate the total price of the units that cost $4.50.   22.____

    A. $315   B. $31,500   C. $3,150   D. $2,800

23. Calculate the total price of the units that cost $3.75.   23.____

    A. $2062.50 B. $12,000   C. $120   D. $1,200

24. Calculate the total price of the units that cost $2.75.   24.____

   A. $1,512.50   B. $15,125   C. $151.25   D. $550

25. Calculate the total price of the units that cost $1.90.   25.____

   A. $90.25   B. $9025   C. $902.50   D. $475

26. Calculate the average cost per unit.   26.____

   A. $27   B. $33.10   C. $0.30   D. $3.31

27. The interest on a promissory note is recorded at which of the following times?   27.____

   A. When the debt is incurred
   B. At the end of the accounting period
   C. When the note is paid
   D. At the beginning of each month

28. The interest on a promissory note begins accruing at which of the following times?   28.____

   A. When the debt is incurred
   B. At the end of the accounting period
   C. When the note is paid
   D. At the beginning of each month

29. The maturity value of an interest-bearing note is the   29.____

   A. interest accrued on the note plus a service charge imposed by the lender
   B. interest accrued on the note
   C. face value of the note
   D. principal of the note plus interest

30. A cash receipts journal is used to record the   30.____

   A. number of cash sales a business makes
   B. number of credit sales a business makes
   C. collection of cash made by the business
   D. expenditure of cash made by the business

31. Calculate the interest on a promissory note issued for $3,000 at an interest rate of 8%, due in 360 days. (Assume a banking year of 360 days.)   31.____

   A. $300   B. $240   C. $60   D. $360

32. Calculate the total payment due for a promissory note issued for $1,000 at an interest rate of 10%, due in 90 days. (Assume a banking year of 360 days.)   32.____

   A. $25   B. $1050   C. $1000   D. $1025

33. Calculate the total payment due for a promissory note issued for $5,000 at an interest rate of 6%, due in 60 days. (Assume a banking year of 360 days.)   33.____

   A. $5,050   B. $50   C. $5,000   D. $5,300

34. Calculate the interest on a promissory note issued for $1,700 at an interest rate of 12%, due in 45 days. (Assume a banking year of 360 days.) 34.____

    A. $204   B. $1725.50   C. $25.50   D. $1904

35. Calculate the interest on a promissory note issued for $600 at an interest rate of 9%, due in 90 days. (Assume a banking year of 360 days.) 35.____

    A. $13.50   B. $135   C. $54   D. $540

KEY (CORRECT ANSWERS)

1. B		16. C	
2. C		17. D	
3. A		18. B	
4. B		19. A	
5. B		20. D	
6. C		21. A	
7. D		22. C	
8. D		23. D	
9. D		24. A	
10. A		25. C	
11. B		26. D	
12. C		27. C	
13. D		28. A	
14. B		29. D	
15. A		30. C	

31. B
32. D
33. A
34. C
35. A

EXAMINATION SECTION
TEST 1

DIRECTIONS: Each question or incomplete statement is followed by several suggested answers or completions. Select the one that BEST answers the question or completes the statement. *PRINT THE LETTER OF THE CORRECT ANSWER IN THE SPACE AT THE RIGHT.*

1. Assume that you are one of several clerks employed in the office of a city department. Members of the public occasionally visit the office to obtain information. Because your desk is nearest the entrance to the office, most of these visitors direct their inquiries to you. One morning when every one including yourself is busy, a visitor enters the office and asks you for some readily available information.
Of the following, the BEST action for you to take is to

    A. disregard his question in the hope that he will direct his inquiry to another clerk
    B. inform him politely that you are busy now and ask him to return in the afternoon
    C. give him the requested information concisely but courteously and then continue with your work
    D. advise him to write a letter to your department so that the information can be sent to him

1.____

2. As a clerk in the payroll bureau of a city department, you have been assigned the task of checking several payroll sheets. Your supervisor has informed you that these payroll sheets are needed by another department and must be sent to that department by 4 P.M. that day. After you have worked for a few hours, you realize that you will be unable to complete this assignment on time.
Of the following, the BEST action for you to take first is to

    A. ask a co-worker to help you
    B. check only those payroll sheets which you think are most important
    C. make sure that the payroll sheets which have been checked are sent out on time
    D. inform your supervisor of the situation

2.____

3. The switchboard operator of Department X refers a call to the department's Personnel Bureau. Miss Jones, a clerk in the Personnel Bureau, answers this call.
Of the following ways of answering this call, the MOST acceptable one is for Miss Jones to say

    A. "Hello."
    B. "Personnel Bureau, Miss Jones speaking."
    C. "Miss Jones speaking. To whom do you wish to speak?!'
    D. "Hello. This is Miss Jones of Department X."

3.____

4. A clerk in the mailing division of a large city department should be acquainted with the functions of the other divisions of the department CHIEFLY because he will be

    A. able to answer questions asked by visitors regarding the department
    B. more conscientious in doing his work if he knows that other divisions of the department perform important functions
    C. in a better position to make suggestions for improving the work of the various divisions of the department
    D. able to determine the proper division to which mail is to be forwarded

4.____

5. The central filing unit of a certain city department keeps in its files records used by the various bureaus in connection with their daily work.
It is desirable for the clerks in this filing unit to refile records as soon as possible after they have been returned by the different bureaus CHIEFLY because

   A. records which are needed can be located most easily if they have been filed
   B. such procedure develops commendable work habits among the employees
   C. records which are not filed immediately are usually filed incorrectly
   D. the accumulation of records to be filed gives the office a disorderly appearance

6. The active and inactive file material of an office is to be filed in several four-drawer filing cabinets.
Of the following, the BEST method of filing the material is, in general, to

   A. keep inactive material in the upper drawers of the file cabinet so that such material may be easily removed for disposal
   B. keep active material in the upper drawers so that the amount of stooping by clerks using the files is reduced to a minimum
   C. assign drawers in the file cabinets alternately to active and to inactive material so that file material can be transferred easily from the active to the inactive files
   D. assign file cabinets alternately to active and to inactive material so that cross-references between the two types of material can be easily made

7. Of the following, the BEST reason for using form letters is that they

   A. enable an individual to transmit unpleasant or disappointing communications in a gentle and sympathetic manner
   B. present the facts in a terse, business-like manner
   C. save the time of both the dictator and the typist in answering letters dealing with similar matters
   D. are flexible and can be easily changed to meet varying needs and complex situations

8. City agencies use either window envelopes or plain envelopes in mailing their correspondence, depending upon the type of mail being sent out.
When a mail clerk uses a window envelope rather than a plain envelope, he should be especially careful in

   A. sealing and stamping the envelope
   B. affixing the correct amount of postage
   C. folding and inserting the communication
   D. checking the return address

9. As a mail clerk, you have been instructed to make sure that an important letter is received by the person to whom it is addressed.

   Of the following, the BEST action for you to take is to send the letter by
   A. registered mail   B. special delivery
   C. air mail   D. first-class mail

10. In filing, a clerk must often attach several papers together before placing them in the files. Usually, the MOST desirable of the following methods of attaching these papers is to

    A. pin them together
    B. staple them together
    C. attach them with a paper clip
    D. glue them together

10._____

11. It is a common practice in answering a letter of inquiry to make a copy of the reply. A clerk should know that, of the following, the BEST procedure to follow with the copy is to

    A. file it with the letter it answers
    B. file it alphabetically in a separate copy file
    C. file it chronologically in a separate copy file and destroy the copy after thirty days
    D. enclose it with the letter of reply

11._____

12. Suppose that much of the work of your office involves computation of statistical data. This computation is being done without the use of adding machines. You believe the work could be done more efficiently if adding machines were used.
    Of the following, the BEST action for you to take is to

    A. carry out your assignments without comment, since it is not your function to recommend revisions in office practices
    B. have other clerks who agree with you sign a memorandum requesting your supervisor to install adding machines
    C. obtain concrete facts to support your views and then take this matter up with your supervisor
    D. point out to your supervisor every time an error is made that it would not have occurred if adding machines had been used

12._____

13. A clerk employed in the central file section of a city department has been requested to obtain a certain card which is kept in an alphabetic file containing several thousand cards. The clerk finds that this card is not in its proper place and that there is no out card to aid him in tracing its location.
    Of the following, the course of action which would be LEAST helpful to him in locating the missing card would be for him to

    A. secure the assistance of his superior
    B. look at several cards filed immediately before and after the place where the missing card should be filed
    C. ask the other clerks in the file section whether they have this card
    D. prepare an out card and place it where the missing card should be filed

13._____

14. The one of the following types of computer software which requires the use of spreadsheets is

    A. Excel   B. Acrobat   C. Outlook   D. Safari

14._____

15. A clerk assigned to file correspondence in a subject file would be MOST concerned with the
    A. name of the sender   B. main topic of the correspondence
    C. city and state of the sender D. date of the correspondence

15._____

16. Assume that you are responsible for storing and distributing supplies in a city department. The one of the following factors which you should consider LEAST important in selecting a suitable place in the stock room for storing a particular item is

    A. the frequency of requests for it
    B. its perishability
    C. its size
    D. the importance of the bureaus using it

17. A clerk in charge of the supply room of a city department notices that one of the bureaus is asking for considerably more stationery than it has requested in the past.
    For him to inquire into the reasons for the increased demand would be

    A. *desirable*; the amount of stationery used by a bureau should remain constant
    B. *undesirable*; the increased demand may be due to waste, a condition beyond his control
    C. *desirable*; he will be better able to estimate future needs for stationery
    D. *undesirable*; he may be accused of meddling in matters which do not concern him

18. One of the first things an executive usually looks for when he arrives in the morning is his mail.
    Of the following, the MOST valid implication on the basis of this statement is that

    A. letters addressed to an executive should be answered in the order in which they are received
    B. whenever possible, mail for an executive should be on his desk before his arrival in the morning
    C. letters to a city department should be addressed to the department head
    D. the first task of an executive upon his arrival in the morning should be to answer his mail

19. Persons in the employ of a public agency generally come into contact with many people outside of working hours. In these contacts, the government employee represents to the public the quality, competence, and stature of public employees as a group.
    The one of the following statements which is the MOST valid implication of the above observation is that

    A. the responsibilities of a public employee cease after office hours
    B. government employees who come into contact with the public during working hours should be more efficient than those who have no contact with the public
    C. a public employee, by his behavior during social activities, can raise the prestige of public employment
    D. employees of a private company have greater responsibilities during office hours than employees of a public agency

20. Filing, in a way, is a form of recording.

    The one of the following which BEST explains this statement is that
    A. no other records are required if a proper filing system is used
    B. important records should, as a rule, be kept in filing cabinets
    C. a good system of record keeping eliminates the necessity for a filing system
    D. filing a letter or document is, in effect, equivalent to making a record of its contents

21. In standardizing clerical tasks, one should attempt to eliminate the undesirable elements and to retain the desirable ones.
Of the following, the MOST valid implication of the above statement is that

    A. a task containing undesirable elements cannot be standardized
    B. standardized clerical tasks should not contain any unnecessary steps
    C. interesting clerical tasks are easier to standardize than monotonous clerical tasks
    D. a clerical task cannot have both desirable and undesirable elements

22. The efficiency of office workers in affected by the quality of the services provided to facilitate their work.
The one of the following statements which is the BEST illustration of the above judgment is that

    A. a poorly run mail room will hamper the work of the office staff
    B. continual tardiness on the part of an office worker will be reflected in the erformance of his work
    C. a system of promoting office workers through competitive examinations will increase their efficiency
    D. the use of a time clock will improve the quality of the work performed

23. In elections held in various states, the provisions relating to veterans' preference have been amended to conform with Federal practice.
In general, the MOST accurate statement regarding veterans' preference in civil service open competitive examinations for original appointment is that

    A. disabled veterans passing an examination will be given 10 additional points and non-disabled veterans passing an examination will be given 5 additional points
    B. disabled veterans passing an examination will be placed on top of the eligible list; non-disabled veterans will be placed after them; and non-veterans will be placed last on the list
    C. only disabled veterans will be given 5 additional points; no additional points will be given to nondisabled veterans
    D. the granting of additional points to all disabled and non-disabled veterans will be discontinued

24. Suppose that you are assigned to the information desk in your department. Your function is to give information to members of the public who telephone or call in person. It is a busy period of the year. There is a line of seventeen people waiting to speak to you. Because you are constantly being interrupted by telephone calls for information, however, you are unable to give any attention to the people waiting on line. The line is increasing in length.
Of the following, the BEST action for you to take is to

    A. explain courteously to the people on line that you will probably be unable to help them
    B. advise the people at the end of the line that you will probably not reach them for some time and suggest that they come back when you are less busy
    C. ask the switchboard operator to answer telephone requests for information herself instead of putting the calls on your extension
    D. ask your supervisor to assign another clerk to answer telephone calls so that you can give your full attention to the people on line

25. Suppose that you are acting as the receptionist in your department. A man comes up to you, introduces himself as Mr. Smith, and says that he has an appointment with Mr. Brown, one of the clerks in your department. You know that Mr. Brown has been called out of the office for a few days on important business. Upon learning of Mr. Brown's absence, Mr. Smith asks whether someone else can help him. For you to telephone Mr. Brown's office and ask whether some other clerk there can help Mr. Smith would be WISE mainly because

    A. Mr. Smith's business is probably confidential
    B. another clerk has probably been assigned to do Mr. Brown's work in Mr. Brown's absence
    C. Mr. Brown may return unexpectedly
    D. it is uncertain whether Mr. Smith actually does have an appointment with Mr. Brown

26. One of your duties may be to deliver copies of administrative orders to administrators in your department. It is not necessary for an administrator to sign a receipt for his copy of an order. One of the administrators to whom you are requested to deliver a copy of an order is not at his desk when you make your usual tour of the office. Of the following, the BEST action for you to take is to

    A. keep this order until a later order is issued and then deliver both orders at the same time
    B. wait until you meet the administrator in the corridor and give him his copy in person
    C. leave a note on the administrator's desk requesting him to call
    D. leave the administrator's copy of the order on his desk

27. One of your duties may be to deliver inter-office mail to all of the offices in the department in which you work.
    Of the following, the BEST procedure for you to follow before you deliver the letters is, in general, to arrange them on the basis of the

    A. offices to which the letters are to be delivered
    B. dates on which the letters were written
    C. specific persons by whom the letters were signed
    D. offices from which the letters come

28. The population census of the country is undertaken every ten years by the United States Department of
    A. Labor   B. the Treasury   C. Commerce   D. the Interior

29. Of the following pairs of offices in the Federal government, the pair which is held by the same individual is
    A. Secretary of Defense and Secretary of the Army
    B. Chairman of the Atomic Energy Commission and Chairman of the Tennessee Valley Authority
    C. Chief Justice of the United States Supreme Court and Attorney General
    D. Vice President of the United States and President of the Senate

30. A clerk who is familiar with the organization and activities of the United Nations should know, of the following statements, the MOST accurate one is that
    A. the permanent headquarters of the United Nations is in Geneva, Switzerland
    B. devaluation of the currency of a member nation must be approved by the United Nations General Assembly
    C. there are five permanent members on the United Nations Security Council
    D. the Economic Cooperation Administration (ECA) is under the jurisdiction of the United Nations Secretary General

31. In anticipation of a seasonal increase in the amount of work to be performed by his division, a division chief prepared the following list of additional temporary employees needed by his division and the amount of time they would be employed:

    26 cashiers, each at $24,000 a year, for 2 months
    15 laborers, each at $85.00 a day, for 50 days
    6 clerks, each at $21,000 a year, for 3 months

The total approximate cost for this additional personnel would be MOST NEARLY

    A. $200,000   B. $250,000   C. $500,000   D. $600,000

31.____

32. A calculating machine company offered to sell a city agency 4 calculating machines at a discount of 15% from the list price, and to allow the agency $85 for each of its two old machines. The list price of the new machines is $625 per machine.
If the city agency accepts this offer, the amount of money it will have to provide for the purchase of these four machines is

    A. $1,785   B. $2,295   C. $1,955   D. $1,836

32.____

33. A stationery buyer was offered bond paper at the following price scale:
    $2.86 per ream for the first 1,000 reams
    $2.60 per ream for the next 4,000 reams
    $2.40 per ream for each additional ream beyond 5,000 reams
If the buyer ordered 10,000 reams of paper, the average cost per ream, computed to the NEAREST cent, was

    A. $2.48   B. $2.53   C. $2.62   D. $2.72

33.____

34. A clerk has 5.70% of his salary deducted for his retirement pension.
If this clerk's annual salary is $20,400, the monthly deduction for his retirement pension is

    A. $298.20   B. $357.90   C. $1,162.80   D. $96.90

34.____

35. In a certain bureau, two-thirds of the employees are clerks and the remainder is typists.
If there are 90 clerks, then the number of typists in this bureau is

    A. 135   B. 45   C. 120   D. 30

35.____

Questions 36-45.

DIRECTIONS: Assume that the code tables shown below are used by a city department in classifying its employees. Questions 36 to 45 are to be answered on the basis of these tables. In accordance with these code tables, each employee in the department is assigned a code number consisting of ten digits arranged from left to right in the following order:
    I. Division in which Employed
    II. Title of Position
    III. Annual Salary
    IV. Age
    V. Number of Years Employed in Department

Example: A clerk is 21 years old, has been employed in the department for three years, and is working in the Supply Division at a yearly salary of $25,000. His code number should be 90-115-13-02-2.

Questions 36-45.

DIRECTIONS: Assume that the code tables shown below are used by a city department in classifying its employees. Questions 36 to 45 are to be answered on the basis of these tables. In accordance with these code tables, each employee in the department is assigned a code number consisting of ten digits arranged from left to right in the following order:

- VI. Division in which Employed
- VII. Title of Position
- VIII. Annual Salary
- IX. Age
- X. Number of Years Employed in Department

Example: A clerk is 21 years old, has been employed in the department for three years, and is working in the Supply Division at a yearly salary of $25,000. His code number should be 90-115-13-02-2.

DEPARTMENTAL CODE

TABLE I		TABLE II		TABLE III		TABLE IV		TABLE V	
Code No.	Division in Which Employed	Code No.	Title of position	Code No.	Annual Salary	Code No.	Age	Code No.	No. of years Employed in Dept.
10-	Accounting Division	115-	Clek	11-	$18,000 or less	01-	under 20 yrs	1-	less than 1 yrs
20-	Construction Division	155-	Typist	12-	$18,001 to $24,000	02-	20 to 29 yrs	2-	1 to 5 yrs
30-	Engineering Division	175-	Stenographer	13-	$24,001 to $30,000	03-	30 to 39 yrs	3-	6 to 10 yrs
40-	Information Division	237-	Book-Keeper	14-	$30,001 to $36,000	04-	40 to 49 yrs	4-	11 to 15 yrs
50-	Maintenance Division	345-	Statistician	15-	$36,001 to $45,000	05-	50 to 59 yrs	5-	16 to 25 yrs
60-	Personnel Division	545-	Store-Keeper	16-	$45,001 to $60,000	06-	62 to 69 yrs	6-	26 to 35 yrs
70-	Record Division	633-	Drafts-Man	17-	$60,001 to $70,000	07-	70 yrs or over	7-	36 yrs. or over
80-	Research Division	665-	Civil-Engineer	18-	$70,001 or over				
90-	Supply Division	865-	Machinist						
		915-	Porter						

36. A draftsman employed in the Engineering Division yearly salary of $34,800 is 36 years old and has employed in the department for 9 years.
He should be coded

    A. 20-633-13-04-3
    B. 50-665-14-04-4
    C. 30-865-13-03-4
    D. 30-633-14-03-3

36._____

37. A porter employed in the Maintenance Division at a yearly salary of $28,800 is 52 years old and has been employed in the department for 6 years.
He should be coded

    A. 50-915-12-03-3
    B. 90-545-12-05-3
    C. 50-915-13-05-3
    D. 90-545-13-03-3

37._____

38. Richard White, who has been employed in the department for 12 years, receives $50,000 a year as a civil engineer in the Construction Division. He is 38 years old.
He should be coded
    A. 20-665-16-03-4
    B. 20-665-15-02-1
    C. 20-633-14-04-2
    D. 20-865-15-02-5

38._____

39. An 18-year-old clerk appointed to the department six months ago is assigned to the Record Division. His annual salary is $21,600.
He should be coded

    A. 70-115-11-01-1
    B. 70-115-12-01-1
    C. 70-115-12-02-1
    D. 70-155-12-01-1

39._____

40. An employee has been coded 40-155-12-03-3.
Of the following statements made regarding this employee, the MOST accurate one is that he is

    A. a clerk who has been employed in the department for at least 6 years
    B. a typist who receives an annual salary which does not exceed $24,000
    C. under 30 years of age and has been employed in the department for at least 11 years
    D. employed in the Supply Division at a salary which exceeds $18,000 per annum

40._____

41. Of the following statements regarding an employee who is coded 60-175-13-01-2, the LEAST accurate statement is that this employee
    A. is a stenographer in the Personnel Division
    B. has been employed in the department for at least one year
    C. receives an annual salary which exceeds $24,000
    D. is more than 20 years of age

41._____

42. The following are the names of our employees of the department with their code numbers:

James Black, 80-345-15-03-4;
William White, 30-633-14-03-4;
Sam Green, 80-115-12-02-3;
John Jones, 10-237-13-04-5.

42._____

If a salary increase is to be given to the employees who have been employed in the department for 11 years or more and who earn less than $36,001 a year, the two of the above employees who will receive a salary increase are

- A. John Jones and William White
- B. James Black and Sam Green
- C. James Black and William White
- D. John Jones and Sam Green

43. Code number 50-865-14-02-6, which has been assigned to a machinist, contains an obvious inconsistency. This inconsistency involves the figures

    A. 50-865   B. 865-14   C. 14-02   D. 02-6

44. Ten employees were awarded merit prizes for outstanding service during the year. Their code numbers were:

    80-345-14-04-4   40-155-12-02-2
    40-155-12-04-4   10-115-12-02-2
    10-115-13-03-2   80-115-13-02-2
    80-175-13-05-5   10-115-13-02-3
    10-115-12-04-3   30-633-14-04-4

    Of these ten outstanding employees, the number who were clerks employed in the Accounting Division at a salary ranging from $24,001 to $30,000 per annum is

    A. 1   B. 2   C. 3   D. 4

45. The MOST accurate of the following statements regarding the ten outstanding employees listed in Question 44 above is that

    A. fewer than half of the employees were under 40 years of age
    B. there were fewer typists than stenographers
    C. four of the employees were employed in the department 11 years or more
    D. two of the employees in the Research Division receive annual salaries ranging from $30,001 to $36,000

Questions 46-55.

DIRECTIONS: Questions 46 to 55 consist of groups of names. For each group, three different filing arrangements of the names in the group are given. In only one of these arrangements are the names in correct filing order according to the alphabetic filing rules which are given below. For each group, select the one arrangement, lettered A, B, or C, which is CORRECT and indicate in the space at the right the letter which corresponds to the CORRECT arrangement of names.

RULES FOR ALPHABETIC FILING

NAMES OF INDIVIDUALS

(1) The names of individuals are to be filed in strict alphabetic order. The order of filing is: first according to the last name; then according to the first name or initial; and finally according to the middle name or initial.

(2) Where two last names are identical, the one with an initial instead of the first name precedes the one with a first name beginning with the same initial letter. For example: D. Smith and D.J. Smith precede Donald Smith.

(3) Where two individuals with identical last names also have identical first names or initials, the one without a middle name or initial precedes the one with a middle name or initial. For example: D. Smith precedes D.J. Smith, and Donald Smith precedes Donald J. Smith.

(4) Where two individuals with identical last names also have identical first names or initials, the one with an initial instead of the middle name precedes the one with a middle name beginning with the same initial letter. For example: Donald J. Smith precedes Donald Joseph Smith.

<u>NAMES OF BUSINESS ORGANIZATIONS</u>

The names of business organizations are to be filed in alphabetic order as written, except that the names of an organization containing the name of an individual is filed alphabetically according to the name of the individual as described in the above rules. For example: John Burke Wine Co. precedes Central Storage Corp.

<u>ADDITIONAL RULES</u>

(1) Names composed of numerals or of abbreviations of names are to be treated as if the numerals or the abbreviations were spelled out.
(2) Prefixes such as De, Di, O', Le, and La are considered as part of the names they precede.
(3) Names beginning with "Mc" and "Mac" are to be filed as spelled.
(4) The following titles and designations are to be disregarded in filing: Dr., Mr., Jr., Sr., D.D.S., and M.D.
(5) The following are to be disregarded when they occur in the names of business organizations: the, of, and.

SAMPLE ITEM:

ARRANGEMENT A	ARRANGEMENT B	ARRANGEMENT C
Robert Morse	R. Moss	R. T. Morse
Ralph Nixon	R. T. Morse	Robert Morse
R. T. Morse	Ralph Nixon	R. Moss
R. Moss	Robert Morse	Ralph Nixon

The CORRECT arrangement is C; the answer should, therefore, be C

46.
ARRANGMENT A	ARRANGEMENT B	ARRANGEMENT C	46.____
R. B. Stevens	Aled T. Stevens	R.Stevens	
Chas. Stevennson	R. B. Stevens	Robert Stevens, Sr.	
Robert Stevensm, Sr.	Robert Stevens, Sr.	Alfred T. Steven s	
Alfred T. Stevens	Chas. Stevenson	Chas. Stevenson	

47.
ARRANGEMENT A	ARRANGEMENT B	ARRANGEMENT C	47.____
Mr. A. T. Breen	John Brewington	Dr. Otis C. Breen	
Dr. Otis C. Breen	Amelia K. Brewington	Mr. A. T. Breen	
Amelia K Brewington	Dr. Otis C. Breen	John Brewington	
John Brewington	Mr. A. T. Breen	Amelia K. Brewington	

48. ARRANGEMENT A
J. Murphy
J. J. Murphy
John Murphy
John J. Murphy

ARRANGEMENT B
John Murphy
John J. Murphy
J. Murphy
J. J. Murphy

ARRANGEMENT C   48.____
J. Murphy
John Murphy
J. J. Murphy
John J. Murphy

49. ARRANGEMENT A
Anthoney Dibuono
George Burns, Sr
Geo. T. Burns, Jr.
Alan J. Byrnes

ARRANGEMENT B
Geo. T. Burns, Jr.
George Burns, Sr.
Anthony DiBuono
Alan J. Byrnes

ARRANGEMENT C   49.____
George Burns, Sr.
George T. Burns, Jr.
Alan J. Byrnes
Anthony DiBuono

50. ARRANGEMENT A
James Macauley
Frank A. Mclowery
Francis Maclaughry
Bernard J. MacMahon

ARRANGEMENT B
James Macauley
Francis Macloughry
Bernard J.Macmahon
Frank A. McLowery

ARRANGEMENT C   50.____
Bernard J. Macmahon
Francis MacLaughry
Frank A. McLowery
James Macauley

51. ARRANGEMENT A
A. J. DiBartolo, Sr.
A. P.DiBartolo
J. A. Bartolo
Anthony J. Bartolo

ARRANGEMENT B
J. A. Bartolo
Anthony J. Bartolo
A. J. DiBartolo
A. J. DiBartolo, Sr.

ARRANGEMENT C   51.____
Anthony J. Bartolo
J. A. Bartolo
A. J. DiBartolo, Sr
A. P. DiBartolo

52. ARRANGEMENT A
Edward Holmes Corp.
Hillside Trust Corp.
Standard Insurance Co.
The Industrial Surety Co

ARRANGEMENT B
Edward Holmes Corp.
Hillside Trust Corp.
The Industrial Surety Co.
Standard Insurance Co.

ARRANGEMENT C   52.____
Hillside Trust Corp.
Edward Holmes Corp
The Industrial Surety Co.
Standard Insurance Co.

53. ARRANGEMENT A
Cooperative Credit Co.
Chas. Cooke Chemical Corp.
John Fuller Baking Co.
4th Avenue Express Co.

ARRANGEMENT B   53.____
Chas, Cooke Chemical Corp.
Cooperative Credit Co.
4th Avenue Express Co.
John Fuller Baking Co.

ARRANGEMENT C
4th Avenue Express Co.
John Fuller Baking Co.
Chas. Cooke Chemical Corp.
Cooperative Credit Co.

54. ARRANGEMENT A
Mr. R. McDaniels
Robert Darling, Jr.
F. L. Ramsey
Charles DeRhone

ARRANGEMENT B
F. L. Ramsey
Mr. R. McDaniels
Charles DeRhone
Robert Darling, Jr.

ARRANGEMENT C   54.____
Robert darling, Jr.
Charles DeRhone
Mr. R. Mcdaniels
F. L. Ramsey

55.

ARRANGEMENT A	ARRANGEMENT B	ARRANGEMENT C	55._____
New York Ominibus Corp.	John J. O'Brien Co.	Nova Scotia Canning Co.	
New York Shipping Co.	New York Ominibus Ciorp.	John J. O'Brien Co.	
Nove Scotia Canning Co.	New York Shipping Co.	New York Ominibus Corp.	
John J. O'Brien Co.	Nove Scotia Canning Co.	New York shipping Co.	

56. He was asked to *pacify* the visitor. The word pacify means MOST NEARLY   56._____

    A. escort   B. interview   C. calm   D. detain

57. To say that a certain document is *authentic* means MOST NEARLY that it is   57._____

    A. fictitious   B. well written   C. priceless   D. genuine

58. A clerk who is *meticulous* in performing his work is one who is   58._____

    A. alert to improved techniques
    B. likely to be erratic and unpredictable
    C. excessively careful of small details
    D. slovenly and inaccurate

59 A pamphlet which is *replete* with charts and graphs is one which   59._____

    A. deals with the construction of charts and graphs
    B. is full of charts and graphs
    C. substitutes illustrations for tabulated data
    D. is in need of charts and graphs

60. His former secretary was *diligent* in carrying out her duties. The word diligent means MOST NEARLY   60._____

    A. incompetent   B. cheerful   C. careless   D. industrious

61. To supepsede means MOST NEARLY to   61._____

    A. take the place of   B. come before
    C. be in charge of   D. divide into equal parts

62. He sent the *irate* employee to the pepsonnel manager. The word *irate* means MOST NEARLY   62._____

    A. irresponsible   B. untidy   C. insubordinate   D. angry

63. An *ambiguous* statement is one which is   63._____
    A forceful and convincing
    B capable of being understood in more than one sense
    C based upon good judgment and sound reasoning processes
    D uninteresting and too lengthy

64. To *extol* means MOST NEARLY to   64._____

    A. summon   B. praise   C. reject   D. withdraw

65. The word *proximity* means MOST NEARLY

   A. similarity   B. exactness   C. harmony   D. nearness

66. His friends had a *detrimental* influence on him. The word detrimental means MOST NEARLY

   A. favorable   B. lasting   C. harmful   D. short-lived

67. The chief inspector relied upon the *veracity* of his inspectors. The word veracity means MOST NEARLY

   A. speed   B. assistance   C. shrewdness   D. truthfulness

68. There was much *diversity* in the suggestions submitted. The word diversity means MOST NEARLY

   A. similarity   B. value   C. triviality   D. variety

69. The survey was concerned with the problem of *indigence*. The word indigence means MOST NEARLY

   A. poverty   B. corruption   C. intolerance   D. morale

70. The investigator considered this evidence to be *extraneous*. The word extraneous means MOST NEARLY

   A. significant
   B. pertinent but unobtainable
   C. not essential
   D. inadequate

71. He was surpised at the *temerity* of the new employee. The word temerity means MOST NEARLY

   A. shyness   B. enthusiasm   C. rashness   D. self-control

72. The term *ex officio* means MOST NEARLY

   A. expelled from office
   B. a former holder of a high office
   C. without official approval
   D. by virtue of office or position

Questions 73-82.

DIRECTIONS: Questions 73 to 82 consist of four words each. One word in each row is INCORRECTLY spelled. For each item, print in the correspondingly numbered space at the right the letter preceding the word which is INCORRECTLY spelled.

73. A. apparent   B. superintendent   C. releive   D. calendar
74. A. foreign   B. negotiate   C. typical   D. discipline
75. A. posponed   B. argument   C. susceptible   D. deficit
76. A. preferred   B. column   C. peculiar   D. equiped

77.	A. exaggerate	B. disatisfied	C. repetition	D. already	77._____
78.	A. livelihood	B. physician	C. obsticle	D. strategy	78._____
79.	A. courageous	B. ommission	C. ridiculous	D. awkward	79._____
80.	A. sincerely	B. abundance	C. negligable	D. elementary	80._____
81.	A. obsolete	B. mischievous	C. enumerate	D. atheletic	81._____
82.	A. fiscel	B. beneficiary	C. concede	D. translate	82._____

Questions 83-97

DIRECTIONS: Each of the following sentences may be classified MOST appropriately under one of the following four categories:
    A. faulty because of incorrect grammar
    B. faulty because of incorrect punctuation
    C. faulty because of incorrect capitalization
    D. correct
Examine each sentence carefully. Then, in the correspondingly numbered space at the right, print the letter preceding the option which is the BEST of the four suggested above. All incorrect sentences contain but one type of error. Consider a sentence correct if it contains none of the types of errors mentioned, even though there may be other eorrect ways of expressing the same thought.

83. Neither of the two administrators are going to attend the conference being held in Washington, D.C.   83._____

84. Since Miss Smith and Miss Jones have more experience than us, they have been given more responsible duties.   84._____

85. Mr. Shaw the supervisor of the stock room maintains an inventory of stationery and office supplies.   85._____

86. Inasmuch as this matter affects both you and I, we should take joint action.   86._____

87. Who do you think will be able to perform this highly technical work?   87._____

88. Of the two employees, John is considered the most competent.   88._____

89. He is not coming home on tuesday; we expect him next week.   89._____

90. Stenographers, as well as typists must be able to type rapidly and accurately.   90._____

91. Having been placed in the safe we were sure that the money would not be stolen   91._____

92. Only the employees who worked overtime last week may leave one hour earlier today.   92._____

93. We need someone who can speak french fluently.   93._____

94. A tall, elderly, man entered the office and asked to see Mr. Brown.   94._____

95. The clerk insisted that he had filed the correspondence in the proper cabinet.   95._____

96. "Will you assist us," he asked? 96.___

97. According to the information contained in the report, a large quantity of paper and envelopes were used by this bureau last year. 97.___

Questions 98-100.

DIRECTIONS: Items 98 to 100 are a test of your proofreading ability.
Each item consists of Copy I and Copy II. You are to assume that Copy I in each item is correct. Copy II, which is meant to be a duplicate of Copy I, may contain some typographical errors.. In each item, compare Copy II with Copy I and determine the number of errors in Copy II. If there are:
no errors, mark your answer A;
1 or 2 errors, mark your answer B;
3 or 4 errors, mark your answer C;
5 or 6 errors, mark your answer D;
7 errors or more, mark your answer E.

98. COPY I 98.___
The Commissioner, before issuing any such license, shall cause an investigation to be made of the premises named and described in such application, to determine whether all the provisions of the sanitary code, building code, state industrial code, state minimum wage law, local laws, regulations of municipal agencies, and other requirements of this article are fully observed. (Section B32-169.0 of Article 23.)

COPY II
The Commissioner, before issuing any such license shall cause an investigation to be made of the premises named and described tn such applecation, to determine whether all the provisions of the sanitary code, bilding code, state tndustrial code, state minimum wage laws, local laws, regulations of municipal agencies, and other requirements of this article are fully observed. (Section E32-169.0 of Article 23.)

99. COPY I 99.___
Among the persons who have been appointed to various agencies are John Queen, 9 West 55th Street, Brooklyn; Joseph Blount, 2497 Durward Road, Bronx; Lawrence K. Eberhardt, 3194 Bedford Street, Manhattan; Reginald L. Darcy, 1476 Allerton Drive, Bronx; and Benjamin Ledwith, 177 Greene Street, Manhattan.

COPY II
Among the persons who have been appointed to various agencies are John Queen, 9 West 56th Street,Brooklyn, Joseph Blount, 2497 Dureward Road, Bronx; Lawrence K. Eberhart, 3194 Belford Street, Manhattan; Reginald L. Darcey, 1476 Allerton drive, Bronx; and Benjamin Ledwith, 177 Green Street, Manhattan.

100. COPY I 100.___
Except as hereinafter provided, it shall be unlawful to use, store or have on hand any inflammable motion picture film in quantities greater than one standard or two sub-standard reels, or aggregating more than two thousand feet in length, or more than ten pounds in weight without the permit required by this section.

COPY II
Except as herinafter provided, it shall be unlawfull to use, store or have on hand any inflammable motion picture film, in quantities greater than one standard or two substandard reels or aggregating more than two thousand feet in length, or more than ten pounds in weight without the permit required by this section.

KEY (CORRECT ANSWERS)

1. C	26. D	51. C	76. D
2. D	27. A	52. C	77. B
3. B	28. C	53. B	78. C
4. D	29. D	54. C	79. B
5. A	30. C	55. A	80. C
6. B	31. A	56. C	81. D
7. C	32. C	57. D	82. A
8. C	33. B	58. C	83. A
9. A	34. D	59. B	84. A
10. B	35. B	60. D	85. B
11. A	36. B	61. A	86. A
12. C	37. C	62. D	87. D
13. D	38. A	63. B	88. A
14. A	39. B	64. B	89. C
15. B	40. B	65. D	90. B
16. D	41. D	66. C	91. A
17. C	42. A	67. D	92. D
18. B	43. D	68. D	93. C
19. C	44. B	69. A	94. B
20. D	45. C	70. C	95. D
21. B	46. B	71. C	96. B
22. A	47. A	72. D	97. A
23. A	48. A	73. C	98. D
24. D	49. C	74. D	99. E
25. B	50. B	75. A	100. E

ARITHMETICAL REASONING

EXAMINATION SECTION

TEST 1

DIRECTIONS: Each question or incomplete statement is followed by several suggested answers or completions. Select the one that BEST answers the question or completes the statement. *PRINT THE LETTER OF THE CORRECT ANSWER IN THE SPACE AT THE RIGHT.*

1. The ABC Corporation had a gross income of $125,500.00 in 2019. Of this, it paid 60% for overhead.
   If the gross income for 2020 increased by $6,500 and the cost of overhead increased to 61% of gross income, how much MORE did it pay for overhead in 2020 than in 2019?
   A. $1,320   B. $5,220   C. $7,530   D. $8,052

   1.____

2. After one year, Mr. Richards paid back a total of $16,950 as payment for a $15,000 loan. All the money paid over $15,000 was simple interest.
   The interest charge was MOST NEARLY
   A. 13%   B. 11%   C. 9%   D. 7%

   2.____

3. A checking account has a balance of $253.36.
   If deposits of $36.95, $210.23, and $7.34 and withdrawals of $117.35, $23.37, and $15.98 are made, what is the NEW balance of the account?
   A. $155.54   B. $351.18   C. $364.58   D. $664.58

   3.____

4. In 2020, the W Realty Company spent 27% of its income on rent.
   If it earned $97,254 in 2020, the amount it paid for rent was
   A. $26,258.58   B. 26,348.58   C. $27,248.58   D. $27,358.58

   4.____

5. Six percent simple annual interest on $2,436.18 is MOST NEARLY
   A. $145.08   B. $145.17   C. $146.08   D. $146.17

   5.____

6. H. Partridge receives a weekly gross salary (before deductions) of $397.50. Through weekly payroll deductions of $13.18, he is paying back a loan he took from his pension fund.
   If other fixed weekly deductions amount to $122.76, how much pay would Mr. Partridge take home over a period of 33 weeks?
   A. $7,631.28   B. $8,250.46   C. $8,631.48   D. $13,117.50

   6.____

7. Mr. Robertson is a city employee enrolled in a city retirement system. He has taken out a loan from the retirement fund and is paying it back at the rate of $14.90 every two weeks.
   In eighteen weeks, how much money will he have paid back on the loan?
   A. $268.20   B. $152.80   C. $134.10   D. $67.05

   7.____

8. In 2019, The Iridor Book Company had the following expenses: rent, $6,500; overhead, $52,585; inventory, $35,700; and miscellaneous, $1,275.
If all of these expenses went up 18% in 2020, what would they TOTAL in 2020?
A. $17,290.80   B. $78,769.20   C. $96,060.00   D. $113,350.80

9. Ms. Ranier had a gross salary of $710.72 paid once every two weeks.
If the deductions from each paycheck are $125.44, $50.26, $12.58, and $2.54, how much money would Ms. Ranier take home in eight weeks?
A. $2,079.60   B. $2,842.88   C. $4,159.20   D. $5,685.76

10. Mr. Martin had a net income of $95,500 in 2019.
If he spent 34% on rent and household expenses, 3% on house furnishings, 25% on clothes, and 36% on food, how much was left for savings and other expenses?
A. $980   B. $1,910   C. $3,247   D. $9,800

11. Mr. Elsberg can pay back a loan of $1,800 from the city employees' retirement system if he pays back $36.69 every two weeks for two full years.
At the end of the two years, how much more than the original $1,800 he borrowed will Mr. Elsberg have paid back?
A. $53.94   B. $107.88   C. $190.79   D. $214.76

12. Mr. Nusbaum is a city employee receiving a gross salary (salary before deductions) of $20,800. Every two weeks, the following deductions are taken out of his salary: Federal Income Tax, $162.84; FICA, $44.26; State Tax, $29.2; City Tax, $13.94; Health Insurance, $3.14.
If Mr. Nusbaum's salary and deductions remained the same for a full calendar year, what would his net salary (gross salary less deductions) be in that year?
A. $6,596.20   B. $14,198.60   C. $18,745.50   D. $20,546.30

13. Add: 8936, 7821, 8953, 4297, 9785, 6579.
A. 45,371   B. 45,381   C. 46,371   D. 46,381

14. Multiply: 987
867
A. 854,609   B. 854,729   C. 855,709   D. 855,729

15. Divide: $59\overline{)321439.0}$
A. 5438.1   B. 5447.1   C. 5448.1   D. 5457.1

16. Divide: $.052\overline{)721}$
A. 12,648.0   B. 12,648.1   C. 12,649.0   D. 12,649.1

17. If the total number of employees in one city agency increased from 1,927 to 2,006 during a certain year, the percentage increase in the number of employees for that year is MOST NEARLY
A. 4%   B. 5%   C. 6%   D. 7%

18. During a single fiscal year, which totaled 248 workdays, one account clerk verified 1,488 purchase vouchers.
Assuming a normal work week of five days, what is the AVERAGE number of vouchers verified by the account clerk in a one-week period during this fiscal year?
  A. 25   B. 30   C. 35   D. 40

18.____

19. Multiplying a number by .75 is the same as
  A. multiplying it by 2/3
  B. dividing it by 2/3
  C. multiplying it by ¾
  D. dividing it by ¾

19.____

20. In City Agency A, 2/3 of the employees are enrolled in a retirement system. City Agency B has the same number of employees as Agency A and 60% of these are enrolled in a retirement system.
If Agency A has a total of 660 employees, how many MORE employees does it have enrolled in a retirement system than does Agency B?
  A. 36   B. 44   C. 56   D. 66

20.____

21. Net worth is equal to assets minus liabilities.
If, at the end of 2019, a textile company had assets of $98,695.83 and liabilities of $59,238.29, what was its net worth?
  A. $38,478.54   B. $38,488.64   C. $39,457.54   D. $48,557.54

21.____

22. Mr. Martin's assets consist of the following: Cash on hand, $5,233.74; Automobile, $3,206.09; Furniture, $4,925.00; Government Bonds, $5,500.00; and House, $36,69.85.
What are his TOTAL assets?
  A. $54,545.68   B. $54,455.68   C. $55,455.68   D. $55,555.68

22.____

23. If Mr. Mitchell has $627.04 in his checking account and then writes three checks for $241.75, $13.24, and $102.97, what will be his new balance?
  A. $257.88   B. $269.08   C. $357.96   D. $369.96

23.____

24. An employee's net pay is equal to his total earnings less all deductions.
If an employee's total earnings in a pay period are $497.05, what is his net pay if he has the following deductions: Federal Income Tax, $18.79; City Tax, $7.25; Pension, $1.88?
  A. $351.17   B. $351.07   C. $350.17   D. $350.07

24.____

25. A petty cash fund had an opening balance of $85.75 on December 1. Expenditures of $23.00, $15.65, $5.23, $14.75, and $26.38 were made out of this fund during the first 14 days of the month. Then, on December 17, another $38.50 was added to the fund.
If additional expenditures of $17.18, $3.29, and $11.64 were made during the remainder of the month, what was the FINAL balance of the petty cash fund at the end of December?
  A. $6.93   B. $7.13   C. $46.51   D. $91.40

25.____

KEY (CORRECT ANSWERS)

1.	B	11.	B
2.	A	12.	B
3.	B	13.	C
4.	A	14.	D
5.	D	15.	C
6.	C	16.	D
7.	C	17.	A
8.	D	18.	B
9.	A	19.	C
10.	B	20.	B

21. C
22. D
23. B
24. D
25. B

———

5 (#1)

SOLUTIONS TO PROBLEMS

1. ($132,000)(.61) – ($125,500)(.60) = $5,220

2. Interest = $1,950. As a percent, $1950 ÷ 15,000 = 13%

3. New balance = $253.36 + $36.95 + $210.23 + $7.34 - $117.35 - $23.37 - $15.98 = $351.18

4. Rent = ($97,254)(.27) = $26,258.58

5. ($2,436.18)(.06) ≈ $146.17

6. ($397.50 - $13.18 - $122.76) = $8,631.48

7. ($14.90)$(\frac{18}{2})$ = $134.10

8. ($6,500 + $52,585 + $35,700 + $1,275)(1.18) = $113,350.80

9. ($710.72 - $125.44 - $50.26 - $12.58 - $2.54)$(\frac{8}{2})$ = $2,079.60

10. (1 - .34 - .03 - .25 - .36) - $1,800 = $107.88

11. (36.69)(52) - $1,800 = $107.88

12. $20,800 – (26)($162.84+$44.26+$29.72+$13.94+$3.14) = $14,198.60

13. 8,936 + 7,821 + 8,953 + 4,297 + 9,785 + 6,579 = 46,371

14. (987)(867) – 855,729

15. 321,439 ÷ 59 ≈ 5,448.1

16. 721 ÷ .057 ≈ 12,649.1

17. (2,006-1,927) ÷ 1,927 ≈ 4%

18. Let x = number of vouchers. Then, $\frac{x}{5} = \frac{1488}{248}$. Solving, x = 30

19. Multiplying by .75 is equivalent to multiplying by $\frac{3}{4}$

20. (660)$(\frac{2}{3})$ – (660)(.60) = 44

21. Net worth = $98,695.83 - $59,238.29 = $39,457.54

22. Total Assets = $5,233.74 + $3,206.09 + $4,925.00 + $5,500.00) + $36,690.85 = $55,555.68.

23. New balance = $627.04 - $241.75 - $13.24 - $102.97 = $269.08

24. Net pay = $497.05 - $90.32 - $28.74 - $18.79 - $7.25 - $1.88 = $350.07

25. Final balance = $85.75 - $23.00 - $15.65 - $5.23 - $14.75 - $26.38 + $38.50 - $17.18 - $3.29 - $11.64 = $7.13

TEST 2

DIRECTIONS: Each question or incomplete statement is followed by several suggested answers or completions. Select the one that BEST answers the question or completes the statement. *PRINT THE LETTER OF THE CORRECT ANSWER IN THE SPACE AT THE RIGHT.*

1. The formula for computing base salary is: Earnings equals base gross plus additional gross.
   If an employee's earnings during a particular period are in the amounts of $597.45, $535.92, $639.91, and $552.83, and his base gross salary is $525.50 per paycheck, what is the TOTAL of the additional gross earned by the employee during that period?
   A. $224.11   B. $224.21   C. $224.51   D. $244.11

   1.____

2. If a lump sum death benefit is paid by the retirement system in an amount equal to 3/7 of an employee's last yearly salary of $13,486.50, the amount of the death benefit paid is MOST NEARLY
   A. $5,749.29   B. $5,759.92   C. $5,779.92   D. $5,977.29

   2.____

3. Suppose that a member has paid 15 installments on a 28-installment loan. The percentage of the number of installments paid to the retirement system is
   A. 53.57%   B. 53.97%   C. 54.57%   D. 55.37%

   3.____

4. If an employee takes a 1-month vacation during a calendar year, the percentage of the year during which he works is MOST NEARLY
   A. 90.9%   B. 91.3%   C. 91.6%   D. 92.1%

   4.____

5. Suppose that an employee took a leave of absence totaling 7 months during a calendar year.
   Assuming the employee did not take any vacation time during the remainder of that year, the percentage of the year in which he worked is MOST NEARLY
   A. 41.7%   B. 43.3%   C. 46.5%   D. 47.1%

   5.____

6. A member has borrowed $4,725 from her funds in the retirement system. If $3,213 has been repaid, the percentage of the loan which is still outstanding is MOST NEARLY
   A. 16%   B. 32%   C. 48%   D. 68%

   6.____

7. If an employee worked only 24 weeks during the year because of illness, the portion of the year he was out of work was MOST NEARLY
   A. 46%   B. 48%   C. 51%   D. 54%

   7.____

8. If an employee purchased credit for a 16-week period of service which he had prior to rejoining the retirement system, the percentage of a year he purchased credit for was MOST NEARLY
   A. 27.9%   B. 28.8%   C. 30.7%   D. 33.3%

   8.____

9. If an employee contributes 2/11 of his yearly salary to his pension fund account, the percentage of his yearly salary which he contributes is MOST NEARLY
   A. 17.9%   B. 18.2%   C. 18.4%   D. 19.0%

10. In 2018, the maximum amount of income from which social security tax could be withheld (base salary) was $70,500. In 2020, the base salary was $82,500. The 2020 base salary represents a percentage increase over the 2018 base salary of APPROXIMATELY
    A. 15%   B. 16%   C. 17%   D. 18%

11. If 17.5% of an employee's salary is withheld for taxes, the one of the following which is the fraction of the salary withheld is
    A. 3/20   B. 8/35   C. 7/40   D. 4/25

12. If a person withdraws 42% of the funds from his account with the retirement system, the remaining balance represents a fraction of MOST NEARLY
    A. 7/13   B. 5/9   C. 7/12   D. 4/7

13. A property decreases in value from $45,000 to $35,000.
    The percent of decrease is MOST NEARLY
    A. 20.5%   B. 22.2%   C. 25.0%   D. 28.6%

14. The fraction $\frac{487}{101326}$ expressed as a decimal is MOST NEARLY
    A. .0482   B. .00481   C. .0049   D. .00392

15. The reciprocal of the sum of 2/3 and 1/6 can be expressed as
    A. 0.83   B. 1.20   C. 1.25   D. 1.50

16. Total land and building costs for a new commercial property equal $50 per square foot.
    If the investors expect a 10 percent return on their costs, and if total operating expenses average 5 percent of total costs, annual gross rentals per square foot must be AT LEAST
    A. $7.50   B. $8.50   C. $10.00   D. $12.00

17. The formula for computing the amount of annual deposit in a compound interest bearing account to provide a lump sum at the end of a period of years is
    $X = \frac{r \cdot L}{(1+r)^{n-1}}$ (X is the amount of annual deposit, r is the rate of interest, and n is the number of years and L = lump sum).
    Using the formula, the annual amount of the deposit at the end of each year to accumulate $20,000 at the end of 3 years with interest at 2 percent on annual balances is
    A. $6,120.00   B. $6,203.33   C. $6,535.09   D. $6,666.66

3 (#2)

18. An investor sold two properties at $150,000 each. On one he made a 2.5 percent profit. On the other, he suffered a 25 percent loss.
The NET result of his sales was
A. neither a gain nor a loss
B. a $20,000 loss
C. a $75,000 gain
D. a $75,000 loss

18.____

19. A contractor decides to install a chain fence covering the perimeter of a parcel 75 feet wide and 112 feet in depth.
Which one of the following represents the number of feet to be covered?
A. 187   B. 364   C. 374   D. 8,400

19.____

20. A builder estimates he can build an average of 4½ one-family homes to an acre. There are 640 acres to one square mile.
Which one of the following CORRECTLY represents the number of one-family homes the builder would estimate he can build on one square mile?
A. 1,280   B. 1,920   C. 2,560   D. 2,880

20.____

21. $.01059 deposit at 7 percent interest will yield $1.00 in 30 years.
If a person deposited $1,059 at 7 percent interest on April 4, 1991, which one of the following amounts would represent the worth of this deposit on March 31, 2021?
A. $100   B. $1,000   C. $10,000   D. $100,000

21.____

22. A building has an economic life of forty years.
Assuming the building depreciates at a constant annual rate, which one of the following CORRECTLY represents the yearly percentage of depreciation?
A. 2.0%   B. 2.5%   C. 5.0%   D. 7.0%

22.____

23. A building produces a gross income of $200,000 with a net income of $20,000, before mortgage charges and capital recapture. The owner is able to increase the gross income 5 percent without a corresponding increase in operating costs.
The effect upon the net income will be an INCREASE of
A. 5%   B. 10%   C. 12.5%   D. 50%

23.____

24. The present value of $1.00 not payable for 8 years, and at 10 percent interest, is $.4665.
Which of the following amounts represents the PRESENT value of $1,000 payable 8 years hence at 10 percent interest?
A. $46.65   B. $466.50   C. $4,665.00   D. $46,650.00

24.____

25. The amount of real property taxes to be levied by a city is $100 million. The assessment roll subject to taxation shows an assessed valuation of $2 billion.
Which one of the following tax rates CORRECTLY represents the tax rate to be levied per $100 of assessed valuation?
A. $.50   B. $5.00   C. $50.00   D. $500.00

25.____

KEY (CORRECT ANSWERS)

1. A
2. C
3. A
4. C
5. A

6. B
7. D
8. C
9. B
10. C

11. C
12. C
13. B
14. B
15. B

16. A
17. C
18. B
19. C
20. D

21. D
22. B
23. D
24. B
25. B

5 (#2)

SOLUTIONS TO PROBLEMS

1. $597.45 + $535.91 + $639.91 + $552.83 = $2,326.11. Then, $2,326.11 − (4)($525.50) = $224.11

2. Death benefit = ($13,486.50)$(\frac{3}{7})$ ≈ $5,779.92

3. $\frac{15}{28}$ ≈ 53.57%

4. $\frac{11}{12}$ ≈ 91.6% (closer to 91.7%)

5. $\frac{5}{12}$ ≈ 41.7%

6. ($4,725-$3,213) ÷ $4,725 = 32%

7. $\frac{28}{52}$ ≈ 54%

8. $\frac{16}{52}$ ≈ 30.7% (closer to 30.8%)

9. $\frac{2}{11}$ ≈ 18.2%

10. ($82,500 - $70,500) ÷ $70,500 = 17%

11. 17.5% = $\frac{175}{1000}$ = $\frac{7}{40}$

12. 100% - 42% = 58% = $\frac{58}{100}$ = $\frac{29}{50}$, closest to $\frac{7}{12}$ in selections

13. $\frac{\$10,000}{\$45,000}$ ≈ 22.2%

14. 487/101,216 ≈ .00481

15. $\frac{2}{3} + \frac{1}{6} = \frac{5}{6}$ Then, $1 \div \frac{5}{6} = \frac{6}{5}$ = 1.20

16. (.15)($50) = $7.50

17. x = (.02)($20,000)/[(1+.02)^3 − 1] = 400 ÷ .061208 ≈ $6,535.09

18. Sold 150,000, 25% loss = paid 200,000, loss of $50,000 Sold 150,000, 25% profit = paid 120,000, profit of 30,000 − 50,000 + 30,000 = 20,000 (loss)

19. Perimeter = (2)(75) + (2)(112) = 374 ft.

20. (640)(4½) = 2,880 homes

21. (1÷.01059)(1059) = $100,000

22. 1÷4 = .025 = 2.5%

23. New gross income = ($200,000)(X1.05) = $210,000
    Then, ($210,000-$200,000) ÷ $20,000 = 50%

24. Let x = present value of $1,000. Then, $\frac{\$1.00}{\$.4665} = \frac{\$1000}{x}$
    Solving, x = $466.50

25. Let x = tax rate. Then, $\frac{\$100,000,000}{\$2,000,000,000} = \frac{x}{\$100}$
    Solving, x = $5.00

TEST 3

DIRECTIONS: Each question or incomplete statement is followed by several suggested answers or completions. Select the one that BEST answers the question or completes the statement. *PRINT THE LETTER OF THE CORRECT ANSWER IN THE SPACE AT THE RIGHT.*

1. It is found that for the past three years the average weekly number of inspections per inspector ranged from 20 inspections to 40 inspections. 1._____
   On the basis of this information, it is MOST reasonable to conclude that
   A. on the average, 30 inspections per week were made
   B. the average weekly number of inspections never fell below 20
   C. the performance of inspectors deteriorated over the three-year period
   D. the range in average weekly inspections was 60

Questions 2-4.

DIRECTIONS: Questions 2 through 4 are to be answered on the basis of the following information.

The number of students admitted to University X in 2019 from High School Y was 268 students. This represented 13.7 percent of University X's entering freshman classes. In 2020, it is expected that University X will admit 591 students from High School Y, which is expected to represent 19.4 percent of the 2020 entering freshman classes of University X.

2. Which of the following is CLOSEST estimate of the size of University's expected 2020 entering freshman classes? 2._____
   _____ students
   A. 2,000   B. 2,500   C. 3,000   D. 3,500

3. Of the following, the expected percentage of increase from 2019 to 2020 in the number of students graduating from High School Y and entering University X as freshmen is MOST NEARLY 3._____
   A. 5.7%   B. 20%   C. 45%   D. 120%

4. Assume that the cost of processing admission to University X from High School Y in 2019 was an average of $28. Also, that this was 1/3 more than the average cost of processing each of the other 2019 freshmen admissions to University X. 4._____
   Then, the one of the following that MOST closely shows the total processing cost of all 2019 freshman admissions to University X is
   A. $6,500   B. $20,000   C. $30,000   D. $40,000

5. Assume that during the fiscal year 2019-2020, a bureau produced 20% more work units than it produced in the fiscal year 2018-2019. Also assume that during the fiscal year 2019-2020 that bureau's staff was 20% smaller than it was in the fiscal year 2018-2019. 5._____

83

On the basis of this information, it would be MOST proper to conclude that the number of work units produced per staff member in that bureau in the fiscal year 2019-2020 exceeded the number of work units produced per staff member in that bureau in the fiscal year 2018-2019 by which one of the following percentages?
A. 20%   B. 25%   C. 40%   D. 50%

6. Assume that during the following fiscal years (FY), a bureau has received the following appropriations:
   FY 2015-2016 - $200,000
   FY 2016-2017 - $240,000
   FY 2017-2018 - $280,000
   FY 2018-2019 - $390,000
   FY 2019-2020 - $505,000

   The bureau's appropriation for which one of the following fiscal years showed the LARGEST percentage of increase over the bureau's appropriation for the immediately previous fiscal year?
   A. FY 2016-2017   B. FY 2017-2018
   C. FY 2018-2019   D. FY 2010-2020

7. Assume that the number of buses (U_t) required for a given line-haul system serving the Central Business District depends upon roundtrip time (t), capacity of bus (c), and the total number of people to be moved in a peak hour (P) in the major direction, i.e., in the morning and out in the evening.
   The formula for the number of buses required is U_t =
   A. Ptc   B. $\frac{tP}{c}$ C. $\frac{cP}{t}$ D. $\frac{ct}{P}$

8. The area, in blocks, that can be served by a single stop for any maximum walking distance is given by the following formula: $a = 2w^2$. In this formula, a = the area served by a stop and w = maximum walking distance.
   If people will tolerate a walk of up to three blocks, how many stops would be needed to service an area of 288 square blocks?
   A. 9   B. 16   C. 18   D. 27

Questions 9-11.

DIRECTIONS: Questions 9 through 11 are to be answered on the basis of the following information.

In 2019, a police precinct records 456 cases of car thefts, which is 22.6 percent of all grand larcenies. In 2020, there were 560 such cases, which constituted 35% of the broader category.

9. The number of crimes in the broader category in 2020 was MOST NEARLY
   A. 1,600   B. 1,700   C. 1,960   D. 2,800

10. The change from 2019 to 2020 in the number of crimes in the broader category represented MOST NEARLY a
    A. 2.5% decrease
    B. 10.1% increase
    C. 12.5% increase
    D. 20% decrease

    10._____

11. In 2020, one out of every 6 of these crimes was solved.
    This represents MOST NEARLY what percentage of the total number of crimes in the broader category that year?
    A. 5.8
    B. 6
    C. 9.3
    D. 12

    11._____

12. Assume that a maintenance shop does 5 brake jobs to every 3 front-end jobs. It does 8,000 jobs altogether in a 240-day year. In one day, one worker can do 3 front-end jobs or 4 brake jobs.
    About how many workers will be needed in the shop?
    A. 3
    B. 5
    C. 10
    D. 18

    12._____

13. Assume that the price of a certain item declines by 6% one year, and then increases by 5 and 10 percent, respectively, during the next two years.
    What is the OVERALL increase in price over the three-year period?
    A. 4.2
    B. 6
    C. 8.6
    D. 10.1

    13._____

14. After finding the total percent change in a price (TO) over a three-year period, as in the preceding question, one could compute the average annual percent change in the price by using the formula
    A. $(1+TC)^{1/3}$
    B. $\frac{(1+TC)}{3}$
    C. $(1+TC)^{1/3-1}$
    D. $\frac{1}{(1+TC)^{1/3}-1}$

    14._____

15. 357 is 6% of
    A. 2,142
    B. 5,950
    C. 4,140
    D. 5,900

    15._____

16. In 2019, a department bought n pieces of a certain supply item for a total of $x. In 2020, the department bought k percent fewer of the item but had to pay a total of g percent more for it.
    Which of the following formulas is CORRECT for determining the average price per item in 2020?
    A. $100\frac{xg}{nk}$
    B. $\frac{x(100+g)}{n(100-k)}$
    C. $\frac{x(100-g)}{n(100+k)}$
    D. $\frac{x}{n} - 100\frac{g}{k}$

    16._____

17. A sample of 18 income tax returns, each with 4 personal exemptions, is taken for 2019 and 2020. The breakdown is as follows in terms of income:

Average Gross Income (in thousands)	Number of Returns	
	2019	2020
40	6	2
80	10	11
120	2	5

    There is a personal deduction per exemption of $500.
    There are no other expense deductions. In addition, there is an exclusion of $3,000 for incomes less than $50,000 and $2,000 for incomes from $50,000 to $99,999.99. From $100,000 upward there is no exclusion.

    17._____

The average net taxable income for the samples in thousands for 2019 is MOST NEARLY
A. $67   B. $85   C. $10   D. $128

18. In the preceding question, the increase in average net taxable income for the sample (in thousands) between 2019 and 2020 is
A. 16   B. 20   C. 24   D. 34

19. Assume that supervisor S has four subordinates—A, B, C, and D.
The MAXIMUM number of relationships, assuming that all combinations are included, that can exist between S and his subordinates is
A. 28   B. 15   C. 7   D. 4

20. If the workmen's compensation insurance rate for clerical workers is 93 cents per $100 of wages, the total premium paid by a city whose clerical staff earns $8,765,000 is MOST NEARLY
A. $8,150   B. $81,515   C. $87,650   D. $93,765

21. Assume that a budget of $3,240,000,000 for the fiscal year beginning July 1, 2020 has been approved. A city sales tax is expected to provide $1,100,000,000; licenses, fees and sundry revenues ae expected to yield $121,600,000; the balance is to be raised from property taxes. A tax equalization board has appraised all property in the city at a fair value of $42,500,000,000. The council wishes to assess property at 60% of its fair value.
The tax rate would need to be MOST NEARLY _____ per $100 of assessed value.
A. $12.70   B. $10.65   C. $7.90   D. $4.00

22. Men's white linen handkerchiefs cost $12.90 for 3.
The cost per dozen handkerchiefs is
A. $77.40   B. $38.70   C. $144.80   D. $51.60

23. Assume that it is necessary to partition a room measuring 40 feet by 20 feet into eight smaller rooms of equal size.
Allowing no room for aisles, the MINIMUM amount of partitioning that would be needed is _____ feet.
A. 90   B. 100   C. 110   D. 140

24. Assume that two types of files have been ordered: 200 of type A and 100 of type B. When the files are delivered, the buyer discovers that 25% of each type is damaged. Of the remaining files, 20% of type A and 40% of type B are the wrong color.
The total number of files that are the WRONG COLOR is
A. 30   B. 40   C. 50   D. 60

25. In a unit of five inspectors, one inspector makes an average of 12 inspections a day, two inspectors make an average of 10 inspections a day, and two inspectors make an average of 9 inspections a day.
If in a certain week one of the inspectors who makes an average of nine inspections a day is out of work on Monday and Tuesday because of illness and all the inspectors do no inspections for half a day on Wednesday because of a special meeting, the number of inspections this unit can be expected to make in that week is MOST NEARLY

 A. 215 B. 225 C. 230 D. 250

25.____

KEY (CORRECT ANSWERS)

1.	B		11.	A
2.	C		12.	C
3.	D		13.	C
4.	D		14.	C
5.	D		15.	B
6.	C		16.	B
7.	B		17.	A
8.	B		18.	A
9.	A		19.	B
10.	D		20.	B

21.	C
22.	D
23.	B
24.	D
25.	A

SOLUTIONS TO PROBLEMS

1. Since the number of weekly inspections ranged from 20 to 40, this implies that the average weekly number of inspections never fell below 20.

2. 591 ÷ 194 ≈ 3046, closest to 3,000 students

3. (591-268) ÷ 268 = 120%

4. Total processing cost = (268)(28) + (1,688)($21) = $42,952, closest to $40,000. [Note: Since 268 represents 13.7%, total freshman population = 268 ÷ .137 ≈ 1,956. Then, 1,956 − 268 = 1,688]

5. Let x = staff size in 2018-2019. Then, .80x = staff size in 2019-2020. Since the 2019-2020 staff produced 20% more work, this is represented by 1.20. However, to measure the productivity per staff member, the factor 1/.80 = 1.25 must also be used to equate the 2 staffs. Then, (1.20)(1.25) = 1.50. Thus, the 2019-2020 staff produced 50% more than the 2018-2019 staff.

6. The respective percent increases are ≈ 20%, 17%, 39%, 29%. The largest would be, over the previous fiscal year, for the current fiscal year 2018-2019

7. $\frac{P}{c}$ = number of buses needed per hour. If t = time (in hrs.), then U_t = tP.c

8. a = (2)(9) = 18 for 1 stop. Then, 288 ÷ 18 = 15 stops.

9. 560 ÷ .35 = 1600 grand larcenies.

10. 456 ÷ .226 = 2018; 560 ÷ .35 = 1600. Then, (1,600-2,018) ÷ 2,018 = -20% or a 20% decrease.

11. $(\frac{1}{6})(560) = 93\frac{1}{3}$. Then, $93\frac{1}{3}$ ÷ 1,600 = 5.8%

12. There are 5,000 brake jobs and 3,000 front-end jobs in one year.
    5,000 ÷ 4 = 1,250 days, and 1,250 ÷ 240 ≈ 5.2. Also, 3,000 ÷ 3 = 1,000 days, and 1,000 ÷ 240 ≈ 4.2. Total number of workers needed ≈ 5.2 + 4.2 ≈ 10.

13. (.94)(1.05)(1.10) = 1.0857, which represents an overall increase by about 8.6%.

14. Average annual % change = $(1+TC)^{1/3} - 1 = (1.0857)^{1/3} - 1 ≈ 2.8\%$.

15. 357 ÷ .06 = 5,950

16. In 2020, $(h)(1-\frac{k}{100})$ pieces cost $(x)(1 + \frac{g}{100})$ dollars. To calculate the cost for 1 piece (average cost), find the value of $[(x)(1 + \frac{G}{100})] ÷ [(n)(1 - \frac{K}{100})] = [(x)(100+g)/100]$. $[100/\{n(100-k)\}] = [x(100+g)]/[n(100-k)]$

7 (#3)

17.

	#	Deductions Up to 50,000	
40,000	6	2000 3000	40,000-3,000-2,000 = 35,000 x 6
80,000	10	2000 2000	80,000-2,000-2,000 = 76,000 x 10
20,000	2	2000	= 118000 x 2

35,000 x 6 = 210,000 = 210
76,000 x 10 = 760,000 = 760
118,800 x 2 = 236,000 = 236
                       1206

1206 ÷ 18 = 67

18.

2020		Deductions			
40,000	2	2000	3000	35,000 x 2 =	70,000
80,000	11	2000	2000	76,000 x 11 =	836,000
120,000	5	2000		118,000 x 5 =	590,000
					1,496,000

1,496,000/18 = 83,111
83,111 − 67,000 = 16,111 = most nearly 16 (in thousands)

19. We are actually looking for the number of different groups of different sizes involving S. This reduces to $_4C_1 + {_4C_2} + {_4C_2} + {_4C_4} = 4 + 6 + 4 + 1 = 15$. The notation $_nC_r$ means combinations of n things taken R at a time = $[(n)(n-1)(n-2)(...)(n-R+1)]/[(R)(R-1)(...)(1)]$. The 15 groups are: SA, SB, SC, SD, SAB, SAC, SAD, SBC, SBD, SCD, SABC, SABD, SACD, SBCD, SABCD.

20. Let x = total premiums. Then, $\frac{.93}{100} = \frac{X}{8,765,000}$ Solving, x = $81,515

21. The balance, raised from property taxes, = $3,240,000,000 - $1,100,000,000 − $121,600,000 = $2,018,400,000. Now, (60)($42,500,000,000) − $25,500,000. The tax rate per $100 of assessed value = ($2,018,400,000)($100)(/$25,500,000,00 = $7.90.

22. A dozen costs ($12.90)($\frac{12}{3}$) = $51.60.

23. (40(20) ÷ 8 = 100 ft.

24. Total number of wrong-color files = (200)(.75)(.20)+(100)(.75)(.40) = 60

25. Weekly number of inspections = (12×5) + (10×5) + (10×5) + (9×5) + 9×5) = 250
    Subtract: 9 Monday, 9 Tuesday, 25 Wednesday
    Total: 250 − 9 − 9 − 25 = 207
    Closest entry is choice A.

EXAMINATION SECTION

TEST 1

DIRECTIONS: Each question or incomplete statement is followed by several suggested answers or completions. Select the one that BEST answers the question or completes the statement. *PRINT THE LETTER OF THE CORRECT ANSWER IN THE SPACE AT THE RIGHT.*

1. Our number system has a base of
 A. 2 B. 5 C. 10 D. 60

2. To find the average weight of the football team,
 A. add and divide B. multiply
 C. add D. divide the weight of each player

3. The thermometer used to measure the temperature of a school is called
 A. Centigrade B. Fahrenheit
 C. fever thermometer D. gauge

4. The value of a fraction is changed when the same number is _____ to both numerator and denominator.
 A. added
 B. divided
 C. multiplied
 D. reduced to both terms of the fraction

5. Stores buy their merchandise from firms called
 A. commissioners B. retail firms
 C. factories D. wholesale firms

6. The amount of money you borrow is called the
 A. amount B. discount
 C. principal D. bank discount

7. An angle of 75° is called a(n) _____ angle.
 A. acute B. obtuse C. straight D. right

8. The rate of interest could be found by the formula
 A. I = Prt B. r = i/pt C. r = Pt D. I = P/Rt

9. If three sides of one triangle are equal to the three sides of the other, the triangles are
 A. equilateral B. right triangles
 C. scalene D. congruent

10. A rectangular solid could be called a(n) 10._____
    A. plane   B. irregular figure
    C. polygon   D. prism

11. A written promise to repay the face of a loan is a 11._____
    A. refund   B. promissory note
    C. dividend   D. deposit

12. The ^{2} written above the s in the formula As^2 means 12._____
    A. 2s   B. s × s   C. s + s   D. s/2

13. Selling price includes cost plus profit plus 13._____
    A. expenses   B. profit   C. loss   D. net price

14. When numbers are used to express how many or how much of units of measure, they are called 14._____
    A. digits   B. denominate numbers
    C. integers   D. whole numbers

15. The square of a number is that number multiplied by 15._____
    A. two   B. twice the number
    C. four   D. itself

16. When the merchant permits the customer to make a down payment and make regular payments on an article, this form of payment is called 16._____
    A. dues   B. rent
    C. installment buying   D. utility payments

17. Circles that have a common center and different radii are _____ circles. 17._____
    A. equal   B. center   C. congruent   D. concentric

18. The United States standard of measure of length is the 18._____
    A. base 10   B. meter
    C. English system   D. metric system

19. If you put money to work for you, the income you receive is called 19._____
    A. income taxes   B. interest
    C. bank discount   D. sales tax

20. A fraction whose numerator is a fraction and denominator is an integer is a _____ fraction. 20._____
    A. common   B. decimal   C. improper   D. complex

KEY (CORRECT ANSWERS)

1.	C	11.	B
2.	A	12.	B
3.	B	13.	A
4.	A	14.	B
5.	D	15.	D
6.	C	16.	C
7.	A	17.	D
8.	B	18.	C
9.	D	19.	B
10.	D	20.	D

SOLUTIONS TO PROBLEMS

1. 10 is the base of our number system. Ex: $456 = (4)(10^2) + (5)(10) + 6$.

2. To find the average weight, add and divide.

3. Fahrenheit degrees would be used for schools.

4. A fraction will change when the same number is added to both numerator and denominator. Ex: Add 5 to both parts of 2/3 to get /8, and 7/8 ≠ 2/3.

5. Stores buy merchandise from wholesale firms.

6. Principal = amount of money borrowed.

7. 75° is an acute angle since it is less than 90°.

8. R = I/(PT) shows rate in terms of interest, principal, and time.

9. If 3 sides of one triangle match 3 sides of a second triangle, they are congruent (SSS).

10. A rectangular solid is a special kind of prism.

11. Promissory note = written promise to repay a loan.

12. $s^2 = s \times s$

13. Selling price includes cost, profit, and expenses.

14. Denominate numbers express units of measure. Ex: 8 gallons.

15. Square of any number = that number times itself. Ex: $4^2 = 4 \times 4 = 16$.

16. Installment buying = down payment + regular payments. Ex: $1000 down payment + $300 payment per month for 2 years.

17. Concentric circles have a common center but different radii. Diagram appears as: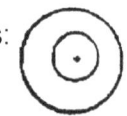

18. The English system is the U.S. standard measure of length. This includes inches, feet, yards, miles, etc.

19. Interest = income received when money is put to work (invested).

20. A complex fraction would contain a fraction within its numerator, denominator, or both.

Ex 1: $\dfrac{\frac{1}{2}}{\frac{1}{3}} = \dfrac{1}{2} \cdot \dfrac{3}{1} = \dfrac{3}{2}$

Ex 2: $\dfrac{1/2}{3} = \dfrac{1}{2} \cdot \dfrac{1}{3} = \dfrac{1}{6}$

Ex 3: $\dfrac{\frac{1}{2}}{3} = \dfrac{1}{1} \cdot \dfrac{3}{2} = \dfrac{3}{2}$

TEST 2

DIRECTIONS: Each question or incomplete statement is followed by several suggested answers or completions. Select the one that BEST answers the question or completes the statement. *PRINT THE LETTER OF THE CORRECT ANSWER IN THE SPACE AT THE RIGHT.*

1. Sally is going to Chicago for a visit. The bus fare is $27.85 one way or a round-trip ticket would be $51.56.
   How much can Sally save by buying a round-trip ticket rather than two one-way tickets?
   A. $4.20
   B. $2.07
   C. $4.14
   D. None of the above

2. The Webster Junior High School collected $226.45 for Junior Red Cross and $420.55 for the Community Chest. There were 850 students in the school.
   To the NEAREST cent, what was the average contribution?
   A. $.76
   B. $.50
   C. $1.00
   D. None of the above

3. Jack borrowed $57.50 from his father and agreed to pay it in twelve monthly payments of $5.00 each.
   How much interest did he pay?
   A. $2.50
   B. $3.50
   C. $7.50
   D. None of the above

4. Joe's mother bought a roast weighing 6 ¾ lbs. at 89¢ a pound.
   How much change did she receive from a $10.00 bill?
   A. $3.99
   B. $5.01
   C. $6.01
   D. None of the above

5. The Athletic Department paid $45 total tax on 1,000 tickets.
   How much tax was this per ticket?
   A. $.22
   B. $.45
   C. 4.5 cents
   D. None of the above

6. Mary bought 4½ yards of lace. She used $1^2/_3$ yards of it on a blouse.
   _____ yards of lace were left.
   A. $3^1/_6$
   B. 3 ½
   C. $2^5/_6$
   D. None of the above

7. The girls are going to make aprons for Junior Red Cross. The pattern calls for ¾ yard of material for one apron.
   They will need _____ yards for 25 aprons.
   A. $33^1/_3$
   B. 18 ¾
   C. 20
   D. None of the above

8. Which city on a world map of standard time zones would be NEAR the 75°W? 8.____
   A. Greenwich B. Sydney
   C. Calcutta D. None of the above

9. John's father made a down payment on a car and has $1,320 left to pay. 9.____
   He pays $55 each month.
   It will take him _____ months to finish the car payments.
   A. 42 B. 24
   C. 18 D. None of the above

10. Pete bought a board 12 ft. 8 in. long from which he wants to make three shelves. 10.____
    Two of the shelves are 2 ft. 8 in. long, and the third shelf is 1 ft. 6 in. long.
    How long will the piece be that is left over?
    A. 5 ft. 8 in. B. 5 ft. 10 in.
    C. 6 ft. 10 in. D. None of the above

11. A factory worker received an increase of 15% in his hourly wages. His former 11.____
    wages were $1.80 per hour.
    How much a week did his wages INCREASE in a forty-hour week?
    A. $21.17 B. $8.00
    C. $10.80 D. None of the above

12. Find the installment price of a washing machine if the down payment is 12.____
    $39.90, the monthly payments are $14.13 for twelve months, and the interest
    charge is $9.86.
    A. $179.52 B. $219.42
    C. $169.56 D. None of the above

13. How many hundreds in 18762? 13.____
    A. 7 B. 87
    C. 187 D. None of the above

14. The football team won 16 games and lost 4 games. 14.____
    What percent of the games played did they win?
    A. 75% B. 80%
    C. 40% D. None of the above

15. The bakery boxed doughnuts one half dozen to a box. 15.____
    They will have _____ full boxes if they fry 500 doughnuts.
    A. 41 B. 83
    C. 82 D. None of the above

16. Jane's parents burn fuel oil. They have used 180 gallons. The gauge indicates 16.____
    the tank is 5/8 full.
    The tank holds _____ gallons.
    A. 255 B. 480
    C. 600 D. None of the above

3 (#2)

17. _____ tiles, each a 9" square, could be laid in one width of a recreation room that is 25 feet long and 16½ feet wide.
    A. 22
    B. 149
    C. 51
    D. None of the above

18. The outside diameter of a wheel on Bob's bicycle is 28 inches. The outside diameter of a wheel on his little brother's bicycle is 21 inches. After traveling a mile, the little brother's wheel will make _____ revolutions more.
    A. 1080
    B. 269.5
    C. 240
    D. None of the above

19. Bill gets 17 ¾ miles per gallon.
    At this rate, he should get _____ miles if he buys 5.6 gallons of gasoline.
    A. 317
    B. 99.4
    C. 85
    D. None of the above

20. The scale drawing of a house is 1 in. = 12 ft.
    If a room is 33 feet long, a _____ inch line should be used on the blueprint to represent that distance.
    A. 2 ¾
    B. 3.3
    C. 2.1`
    D. None of the above

21. A 2-inch gear makes 75 revolutions per minute.
    A 3-inch fear makes _____ rpm at the same rate of speed.
    A. 12 ½
    B. 112 ½
    C. 50
    D. None of the above

22. What is the selling price of a radio that cost the dealer $36 and the margin is 40% of the selling price?
    A. $60
    B. $45
    C. $50.40
    None of the above

23. Mr. Jacks used 35 kwh.
    If the charge is 8¢ a kwh for the first 20 kwh and 5¢ for the remainder, what was the TOTAL charge?
    A. $2.35
    B. $3.35
    C. $4.55
    D. None of the above

24. Druggists use a unit of measurement of weight called the grain. There are *approximately* 437.5 grains in one ounce.
    There are APPROXIMATELY _____ grains in a pound.
    A. 7000
    B. 5252
    C. 73,400
    D. None of the above

25. A gasoline tank is 16 ft. high and has a diameter of 14 ft.
    The tank will hold _____ cubic feet of gasoline (use 22/7 for pi) to the NEAREST 10 cu. ft.
    A. 704
    B. 784
    C. 2460
    D. None of the above

4 (#2)

KEY (CORRECT ANSWERS)

1.	C		11.	C
2.	A		12.	B
3.	A		13.	C
4.	A		14.	B
5.	C		15.	B
6.	C		16.	B
7.	B		17.	A
8.	D		18.	C
9.	B		19.	B
10.	B		20.	A

21. C
22. A
23. A
24. A
25. C

SOLUTIONS TO PROBLEMS

1. Savings = ($27.85)(2) - $51.56 = $4.14

2. Average contribution = ($226.45 + $420.55) ÷ 850 = $647 ÷ 850 ≈ $.76

3. Interest = (12)($5.00) - $57.50 = $2.50

4. $10.00 − (6.75)(.89) = $3.99 change

5. $45 ÷ 1000 = .045 = 4.5 cents tax per ticket

6. 4 1/2 − 1 2/3 = 4 3/6 − 1 4/6 − 1 = 2 5.6 yds, left

7. (3/4)(25) = 18 3/4 yds. needed

8. Refer to world map. None is correct.

9. $1320 ÷ 55 = 24 months

10. 12'8" − 2'8" − 2'8" − 1'6" = 152" − 32" − 32" − 18" = 70" = 5'10"

11. Increase = ($1.80)(.15)(40) = $10.80 per week

12. $39.90 + ($14.13)(12) + $9.96 = $219.42 installment price

13. 18,762 ÷ 100 = 187 with remainder of 62. So, there are 187 hundreds in 18,762.

14. Percent won = 16/20 = 80%

15. 500 ÷ 6 = 83 1/3, which means 83 full boxes + 1/3 of a box

16. 180 gallons represents 3/8 of the entire tank. Thus, the tank's capacity = 180 ÷ 3/8 = 480 gallons

17. 25' = 300" and 16 1/2' = 198". Now, 300 ÷ 9 = 33 1.3 and 198 ÷ 9 = 22. Then the number of tiles that could fit in 1 width = 22. (The actual number of tiles that could fit in the entire room = (22)(33) = 726)

18. 1 revolution of Bob's bicycle = 2π = $(2 \times \frac{22}{7} \times 14)$ = 88"

    1 revolution of his brother's bicycle = 2π = $(2 \times \frac{22}{7} \times 10.5)$ = 66"

19. $(17\frac{3}{4})(5.6) = (17.75)(5.6) = 99.4$ miles

20. 33 ÷ 12 = 2 3/4-inch line needed.

21. Let x = rpm. 2/3 = x/75. Solving, x = 50.
    Note: Size of gear is inversely related to rpm.

22. Let x = selling price. Then, $36 = .60x. Solving, x = $60.

23. Total charge = (.08)(20) + (.05)(15) = $2.35

24. (437.5)(16) = 7000 grains in a pound (approx.)

25. Volume = $(\pi)(7^2)(16) \approx 2460$ cu. ft.

RECORD KEEPING
EXAMINATION SECTION
TEST 1

DIRECTIONS: Each question or incomplete statement is followed by several suggested answers or completions. Select the one that BEST answers the question or completes the statement. *PRINT THE LETTER OF THE CORRECT ANSWER IN THE SPACE AT THE RIGHT.*

Questions 1-15.

DIRECTIONS: Questions 1 through 15 are to be answered on the basis of the following list of company names below. Arrange a file alphabetically, word-by-word, disregarding punctuation, conjunctions, and apostrophes. Then answer the questions.

    A Bee C Reading Materials
    ABCO Parts
    A Better Course for Test Preparation
    AAA Auto Parts Co.
    A-Z Auto Parts, Inc.
    Aabar Books
    Abbey, Joanne
    Boman-Sylvan Law Firm
    BMW Autowerks
    C Q Service Company
    Chappell-Murray, Inc.
    E&E Life Insurance
    Emcrisco
    Gigi Arts
    Gordon, Jon & Associates
    SOS Plumbing
    Schmidt, J.B. Co.

1. Which of these files should appear FIRST?
   A. ABCO Parts
   B. A Bee C Reading Materials
   C. A Better Course for Test Preparation
   D. AAA Auto Parts Co.

2. Which of these files should appear SECOND?
   A. A-Z Auto Parts, Inc.
   B. A Bee C Reading Materials
   C. A Better Course for Test Preparation
   D. AAA Auto Parts Co.

3. Which of these files should appear THIRD?
   A. ABCO Parts
   B. A Bee C Reading Materials
   C. Aabar Books
   D. AAA Auto Parts Co.

4. Which of these files should appear FOURTH?
   A. Aabar Books
   B. ABCO Parts
   C. Abbey, Joanne
   D. AAA Auto Parts Co.

5. Which of these files should appear LAST?
   A. Gordon, Jon & Associates
   B. Gigi Arts
   C. Schmidt, J.B. Co.
   D. SOS Plumbing

6. Which of these files should appear between A-Z Auto Parts, Inc. and Abbey, Joanne?
   A. A Bee C Reading Materials
   B. AAA Auto Parts Co.
   C. ABCO Parts
   D. A Better Course for Test Preparation

7. Which of these files should appear between ABCO Parts and Aabar Books?
   A. A Bee C Reading Materials
   B. Abbey, Joanne
   C. Aabar Books
   D. A-Z Auto Parts

8. Which of these files should appear between Abbey, Joanne and Boman-Sylvan Law Firm?
   A. A Better Course for Test Preparation
   B. BMW Autowerks
   C. Chappell-Murray, Inc.
   D. Aabar Books

9. Which of these files should appear between Abbey, Joanne and C Q Service?
   A. A-Z Auto Parts, Inc.
   B. BMW Autowerks
   C. Choices A and B
   D. Chappell-Murray, Inc.

10. Which of these files should appear between C Q Service Company and Emcrisco?
    A. Chappell-Murray, Inc.
    B. E&E Life Insurance
    C. Gigi Arts
    D. Choices A and B

11. Which of these files should NOT appear between C Q Service Company and E&E Life Insurance?
    A. Gordon, Jon & Associates
    B. Emcrisco
    C. Gigi Arts
    D. All of the above

12. Which of these files should appear between Chappell-Murray, Inc. and Gigi Arts? 12.____
    A. C Q Service Inc., E&E Life Insurance, and Emcrisco
    B. Emcrisco, E&E Life Insurance, and Gordon, Jon & Associates
    C. E&E Life Insurance, and Emcrisco
    D. Emcrisco and Gordon, Jon & Associates

13. Which of these files should appear between Gordon, Jon & Associates and SOS Plumbing? 13.____
    A. Gigi Arts
    B. Schmidt, J.B. Co.
    C. Choices A and B
    D. None of the above

14. Each of the choices lists the four files in their proper alphabetical order EXCEPT 14.____
    A. E&E Life Insurance; Gigi Arts; Gordon, Jon & Associates; SOS Plumbing
    B. E&E Life Insurance; Emcrisco; Gigi Arts; SOS Plumbing
    C. Emcrisco; Gordon, Jon & Associates; SOS Plumbing; Schmidt, J.B. Co.
    D. Emcrisco; Gigi Arts; Gordon, Jon & Associates; SOS Plumbing

15. Which of the choices lists the four files in their proper alphabetical order? 15.____
    A. Gigi Arts; Gordon, Jon & Associates; SOS Plumbing; Schmidt, J.B. Co.
    B. Gordon, Jon & Associates; Gigi Arts; Schmidt, J.B. Co.; SOS Plumbing
    C. Gordon, Jon & Associates; Gigi Arts; SOS Plumbing; Schmidt, J.B. Co.
    D. Gigi Arts; Gordon, Jon & Associates; Schmidt, J.B. Co.; SOS Plumbing

16. The alphabetical filing order of two businesses with identical names is determined by the 16.____
    A. length of time each business has been operating
    B. addresses of the businesses
    C. last name of the company president
    D. no one of the above

17. In an alphabetical filing system, if a business name includes a number, it should be 17.____
    A. disregarded
    B. considered a number and placed at the end of an alphabetical section
    C. treated as though it were written in words and alphabetized accordingly
    D. considered a number and placed at the beginning of an alphabetical section

18. If a business name includes a contraction (such as *don't* or *it's*), how should that word be treated in an alphabetical system? 18.____
    A. Divide the word into its separate parts and treat it as two words
    B. Ignore the letters that come after the apostrophe
    C. Ignore the word that contains the contraction
    D. Ignore the apostrophe and consider all letters in the contraction

19. In what order should the parts of an address be considered when using an alphabetical filing system? 19._____
    A. City or town; state; street name; house or building number
    B. State; city or town; street name; house or building number
    C. House or building number; street name; city or town; state
    D. Street name; city or town; state

20. A business record should be cross-referenced when a(n) 20._____
    A. organization is known by an abbreviated name
    B. business has a name change because of a sale, incorporation, or other reason
    C. business is known by a *coined* or common name which differs from a dictionary spelling
    D. all of the above

21. A geographical filing system is MOST effective when 21._____
    A. location is more important than name
    B. many names or titles sound alike
    C. dealing with companies who have offices all over the world
    D. filing personal and business files

Questions 22-25.

DIRECTIONS: Questions 22 through 25 are to be answered on the basis of the list of items below, which are to be filed geographically. Organize the items geographically and then answer the questions.

      I. University Press at Berkeley, U.S.
     II. Maria Sanchez, Mexico City, Mexico
    III. Great Expectations Ltd. in London, England
    IV. Justice League, Cape Town, South Africa, Africa
     V. Crown Pearls Ltd. in London, England
    VI. Joseph Prasad in London, England

22. Which of the following arrangements of the items is composed according to the policy of: *Continent, Country, City, Firm or Individual Name*? 22._____
    A. V, III, IV, VI, II, I   B. IV, V, III, VI, II, I
    C. I, IV, V, III, VI, II   D. IV, V, III, VI, I, II

23. Which of the following files is arranged according to the policy of: 23._____
    Continent, Country, City, Firm or Individual Name?
    A. South Africa; Africa; Cape Town; Justice League
    B. Mexico; Mexico City; Maria Sanchez
    C. North America; United States; Berkeley; University Press
    D. England; Europe; London; Prasad, Joseph

24. Which of the following arrangements of the items is composed according to the policy of: *Country, City, Firm or Individual Name*?
    A. V, VI, III, II, IV, I
    B. I, V, VI, III, II, IV
    C. VI, V, III, II, IV, I
    D. V, III, VI, II, IV, I

25. Which of the following files is arranged according to a policy of: *Country, City, Firm or Individual Name*?
    A. England; London; Crown Pearls Ltd.
    B. North America; United States; Berkeley; University Press
    C. Africa; Cape Town; Justice League
    D. Mexico City; Mexico; Maria Sanchez

26. Under which of the following circumstances would a phonetic filing system be MOST effective?
    A. When the person in charge of filing can't spell very well
    B. With large files with names that sound alike
    C. With large files with names that are spelled alike
    D. All of the above

Questions 27-29.

DIRECTIONS: Questions 27 through 29 are to be answered on the basis of the following list of numerical files.

   I.   391-023-100
   II. 361-132-170
   III. 385-732-200
   IV. 381-432-150
   V.   391-632-387
   VI. 361-423-303
   VII. 391-123-271

27. Which of the following arrangements of the files follows a consecutive-digit system?
    A. II, III, IV, I
    B. I, V, VII, III
    C. II, IV, III, I
    D. III, I, V, VII

28. Which of the following arrangements follows a terminal-digit system?
    A. I, VII, II, IV, III
    B. II, I, IV, V, VII
    C. VII, VI, V, IV, III
    D. I, IV, II, III, VII

29. Which of the following lists follows a middle-digit system?
    A. I, VII, II, VI, IV, V, III
    B. I, II, VII, IV, VI, V, III
    C. VII, II, I, III, V, VI, IV
    D. VII, I, II, IV, VI, V, III

Questions 30-31.

DIRECTIONS: Questions 30 and 31 are to be answered on the basis of the following information.

  I. Reconfirm Laura Bates appointment with James Caldecort on December 12 at 9:30 A.M.
  II. Laurence Kinder contact Julia Lucas on August 3 and set up a meeting for week of September 23 at 4 P.M.
  III. John Lutz contact Larry Waverly on August 3 and set up appointment for September 23 at 9:30 A.M.
  IV. Call for tickets for Gerry Stanton August 21 for New Jersey on September 23, flight 143 at 4:43 P.M.

30. A chronological file for the above information would be
   A. IV, III, II, I   B. III, II, IV, I   C. IV, II, III, I   D. III, I, II, IV

31. Using the above information, a chronological file for the date September 23 would be
   A. II, III, IV   B. III, I, IV   C. III, II, IV   D. IV, III, II

Questions 32-34.

DIRECTIONS: Questions 32 through 34 are to be answered on the basis of the following information.

  I. Call Roger Epstein, Ashoke Naipaul, Jon Anderson, and Sara Washingon on April 19 at 1:00 P.M. to set up meeting with Alika D'Ornay for June 6 in New York.
  II. Call Martin Ames before noon on April 19 to confirm afternoon meeting with Bob Greenwood on April 20th.
  III. Set up meeting room at noon for 2:30 P.M. meeting on April 19th.
  IV. Ashley Stanton contact Bob Greenwood at 9:00 A.M. on April 20 and set up meeting for June 6 at 8:30 A.M.
  V. Carol Guiland contact Shelby Van Ness during afternoon of April 20 and set up meeting for June 6 at 10:00 A.M.
  VI. Call airline and reserve tickets on June 6 for Roger Epstein trip to Denver on July 8.
  VII. Meeting at 2:30 P.M. on April 19th.

32. A chronological file for all of the above information would be
   A. II, I, III, VII, V, IV, VI   B. III, VII, II, I, IV, V, VI
   C. III, VII, I, II, V, IV, VI   D. II, III, I, VII, IV, V, VI

33. A chronological file for the date of April 19th would be
   A. II, III, VII, I   B. II, III, I, VII   C. VII, I, III, II   D. III, VII, I, II

34. Add the following information to the file, and then create a chronological file for April 20th: VIII. April 20: 3:00 P.M. meeting between Bob Greenwood and Martin Ames.
    A. IV, V, VIII
    B. IV, VIII, V
    C. VIII, V, IV
    D. V, IV, VIII

35. The PRIMARY advantage of computer records over a manual system is
    A. speed of retrieval
    B. accuracy
    C. cost
    D. potential file loss

KEY (CORRECT ANSWERS)

1. B	11. D	21. A	31. C
2. C	12. C	22. B	32. D
3. D	13. B	23. C	33. B
4. A	14. C	24. D	34. A
5. D	15. D	25. A	35. A
6. C	16. B	26. B	
7. B	17. C	27. C	
8. B	18. D	28. D	
9. C	19. A	29. A	
10. D	20. D	30. B	

CLERICAL ABILITIES TEST
EXAMINATION SECTION
TEST 1

DIRECTIONS: Each question or incomplete statement is followed by several suggested answers or completions. Select the one that BEST answers the question or completes the statement. *PRINT THE LETTER OF THE CORRECT ANSWER IN THE SPACE AT THE RIGHT.*

Questions 1-10.

DIRECTIONS: Questions 1 through 10 consist of lines of names, dates, and numbers. For each question, you are to choose the option (A, B, C, or D) in Column II which EXACTLY matches the information in Column I. *PRINT THE LETTER OF THE CORRECT ANSWER IN THE SPACE AT THE RIGHT.*

SAMPLE QUESTION

Column I
Schneider 11/16/75 581932

Column II
A. Schneider 11/16/75 518932
B. Schneider 11/16/75 581932
C. Schnieder 11/16/75 581932
D. Shnieder 11/16/75 518932

The correct answer is B. Only Option B shows the name, date, and number exactly as they are in Column I. Option A has a mistake in the number. Option C has a mistake in the name. Option D has a mistake in the name and in the number. Now answer Questions 1 through 10 in the same manner.

	Column I	Column II	
1.	Johnston 12/26/74 659251	A. Johnson 12/23/74 659251 B. Johston 12/26/74 659251 C. Johnston 12/26/74 695251 D. Johnston 12/26/74 659251	1.____
2.	Allison 1/26/75 9939256	A. Allison 1/26/75 9939256 B. Alisson 1/26/75 9939256 C. Allison 1/26/76 9399256 D. Allison 1/26/75 9993356	2.____
3.	Farrell 2/12/75 361251	A. Farell 2/21/75 361251 B. Farrell 2/12/75 361251 C. Farrell 2/21/75 361251 D. Farrell 2/12/75 361151	3.____

4. Guerrero 4/28/72 105689
    A. Guererro 4/28/72 105689
    B. Guerrero 4/28/72 105986
    C. Guerrero 4/28/72 105869
    D. Guerrero 4/28/72 105689

4.____

5. McDonnell 6/05/73 478215
    A. McDonnell 6/15/73 478215
    B. McDonnell 6/05/73 478215
    C. McDonnell 6/05/73 472815
    D. MacDonell 6/05/73 478215

5.____

6. Shepard 3/31/71 075421
    A. Sheperd 3/31/71 075421
    B. Shepard 3/13/71 075421
    C. Shepard 3/31/71 075421
    D. Shepard 3/13/71 075241

6.____

7. Russell 4/01/69 031429
    A. Russell 4/01/69 031429
    B. Russell 4/10/69 034129
    C. Russell 4/10/69 031429
    D. Russell 4/01/69 034129

7.____

8. Phillips 10/16/68 961042
    A. Philpps 10/16/68 961042
    B. Phillips 10/16/68 960142
    C. Phillips 10/16/68 961042
    D. Philipps 10/16/68 916042

8.____

9. Campbell 11/21/72 624856
    A. Campbell 11/21/72 624856
    B. Campbell 11/21/72 624586
    C. Campbell 11/21/72 624686
    D. Campbel 11/21/72 624856

9.____

10. Patterson 9/18/71 76199176
    A. Patterson 9/18/72 76191976
    B. Patterson 9/18/71 76199176
    C. Patterson 9/18/72 76199176
    D. Patterson 9/18/71 76919176

10.____

Questions 11-15.

DIRECTIONS: Questions 11 through 15 consist of groups of numbers and letters which you are to compare. For each question, you are to choose the option (A, B, C, or D) in Column I which EXACTLY matches the group of numbers and letters given in Column I.

SAMPLE QUESTION

<u>Column I</u>
B92466

<u>Column II</u>
A. B92644
B. B94266
C. A92466
D. B92466

The correct answer is D. Only Option D in Column II shows the group of numbers and letters EXACTLY as it appears in Column I. Now answer Questions 11 through 15 in the same manner.

	Column I		Column II	
11.	925AC5	A.	952CA5	11._____
		B.	925AC5	
		C.	952AC5	
		D.	925CA6	
12.	Y006925	A.	Y060925	12._____
		B.	Y006295	
		C.	Y006529	
		D.	Y006925	
13.	J236956	A.	J236956	13._____
		B.	J326965	
		C.	J239656	
		D.	J932656	
14.	AB6952	A.	AB6952	14._____
		B.	AB9625	
		C.	AB9652	
		D.	AB6925	
15.	X259361	A.	X529361	15._____
		B.	X259631	
		C.	X523961	
		D.	X259361	

Questions 16-25.

DIRECTIONS: Each of questions 16 through 25 consists of three lines of code letters and three lines of numbers. The numbers on each line should correspond with the code letters on the same line in accordance with the table below.

Code Letter	S	V	W	A	Q	M	X	E	G	K
Corresponding Number	0	1	2	3	4	5	5	7	8	9

On some of the lines, an error exists in the coding. Compare the letters and numbers in each question carefully. If you find an error or errors on:
  only one of the lines in the question, mark your answer A;
  any two lines in the question, mark your answer B;
  all three lines in the question, mark your answer C;
  none of the lines in the question, mark your answer D.

SAMPLE QUESTION

WQGKSXG	2489068
XEKVQMA	6591453
KMAESXV	9527061

In the above sample, the first line is correct since each code letter listed has the correct corresponding number. On the second line, an error exists because code letter E should have the number 7 instead of the number 5. On the third line, an error exists because the code letter A should have the number 3 instead of the number 2. Since there are errors in two of the three lines, the correct answer is B. Now answer Questions 16 through 25 in the same manner.

16. SWQEKGA 0247983
    KEAVSXM 9731065
    SSAXGKQ 0036894   16.____

17. QAMKMVS 4259510
    MGGEASX 5897306
    KSWMKWS 9125920   17.____

18. WKXQWVE 2964217
    QKXXQVA 4966413
    AWMXGVS 3253810   18.____

19. GMMKASE 8559307
    AWVSKSW 3210902
    QAVSVGK 4310189   19.____

20. XGKQSMK 6894049
    QSVKEAS 4019730
    GSMXKMV 8057951   20.____

21. AEKMWSG 3195208
    MKQSVQK 5940149
    XGQAEVW 6843712   21.____

22. XGMKAVS 6858310
    SKMAWEQ 0953174
    GVMEQSA 8167403   22.____

23. VQSKAVE 1489317
    WQGKAEM 2489375
    MEGKAWQ 5689324   23.____

24. XMQVSKG 6541098
    QMEKEWS 4579720
    KMEVGKG 9571983   24.____

25. GKVAMEW   88912572   25.____
     AXMVKAE   3651937
     KWAGMAV   9238531

Questions 26-35.

DIRECTIONS: Each of Questions 26 through 35 consists of a column of figures. For each question, add the column of figures and choose the correct answer from the four choices given.

26. 5,665.43   26.____
     2,356.69
     6,447.24
     7,239.65

   A. 20,698.01   B. 21,709.01
   C. 21,718.01   D. 22,609.01

27. 817,209.55   27.____
     264,354.29
      82,368.76
     849,964.89

   A. 1,893.977.49   B. 1,989,988.39
   C. 2,009,077.39   D. 2,013,897.49

28. 156,366.89   28.____
     249,973.23
     823,229.49
      56,869.45

   A. 1,286,439.06   B. 1,287,521.06
   C. 1,297,539.06   D. 1,296,421.06

29.   23,422.15   29.____
     149,696.24
     238,377.53
      86,289.79
     505,533.63

   A. 989,229.34   B. 999,879.34
   C. 1,003,330.34   D. 1,023,329.34

30. 2,468,926.70
    656,842.28
      49,723.15
    832,369.59

    A. 3,218,062.72   B. 3,808,092.72
    C. 4,007,861.72   D. 4,818,192.72

30.____

31.   524,201.52
   7,775,678.51
   8,345,299.63
  40,628,898.08
  31,374,670.07

    A. 88,646,647.81   B. 88,646,747.91
    C. 88,648,647.91   D. 88,648,747.81

31.____

32. 6,824,829.40
    682,482.94
  5,542,015.27
    775,678.51
  7,732,507.25

    A. 21,557,513.37   B. 21,567,513.37
    C. 22,567,503.37   D. 22,567,513.37

32.____

33. 22,109,405.58
   6,097,093.43
   5,050,073.99
   8,118,050.05
   4,313,980.82

    A. 45,688,593.87   B. 45,688,603.87
    C. 45,689,593.87   D. 45,689,603.87

33.____

34. 79,324,114.19
  99,848,129.74
  43,331,653.31
  41,610,207.14

    A. 264,114,104.38   B. 264,114,114.38
    C. 265,114,114.38   D. 265,214,104.38

34.____

35. 33,729,653.94
     5,959,342.58
    26,052,715.47
     4,452,669.52
     7,079,953.59

    A. 76,374,334.10   B. 76,375,334.10
    C. 77,274,335.10   D. 77,275,335.10

Questions 36-40.

DIRECTIONS: Each of Questions 36 through 40 consists of a single number in Column I and four options in Column II. For each question, you are to choose the option (A, B, C, or D) in Column II which EXACTLY matches the number in Column I.

SAMPLE QUESTION

Column I
5965121

Column II
A. 5956121
B. 5965121
C. 5966121
D. 5965211

The correct answer is B. Only Option B shows the number EXACTLY as it appears in Column I. Now answer Questions 36 through 40 in the same manner.

Column I
36. 9643242

Column II
A. 9643242
B. 9462342
C. 9642442
D. 9463242

37. 3572477

A. 3752477
B. 3725477
C. 3572477
D. 3574277

38. 5276101

A. 5267101
B. 5726011
C. 5271601
D. 5276101

39. 4469329

A. 4496329
B. 4469329
C. 4496239
D. 4469239

40. 2326308　　　A. 2236308　　　40._____
　　　　　　　　 B. 2233608
　　　　　　　　 C. 2326308
　　　　　　　　 D. 2323608

KEY (CORRECT ANSWERS)

1.	D	11.	B	21.	A	31.	D
2.	A	12.	D	22.	C	32.	A
3.	B	13.	A	23.	B	33.	B
4.	D	14.	A	24.	D	34.	A
5.	B	15.	D	25.	A	35.	C
6.	C	16.	D	26.	B	36.	A
7.	A	17.	C	27.	D	37.	C
8.	C	18.	A	28.	A	38.	D
9.	A	19.	D	29.	C	39.	B
10.	B	20.	B	30.	C	40.	C

TEST 2

DIRECTIONS: Each question or incomplete statement is followed by several suggested answers or completions. Select the one that BEST answers the question or completes the statement. *PRINT THE LETTER OF THE CORRECT ANSWER IN THE SPACE AT THE RIGHT.*

Questions 1-5.

DIRECTIONS: Each of Questions 1 through 5 consists of a name and a dollar amount. In each question, the name and dollar amount in Column II should be an EXACT copy of the name and dollar amount in Column I. If there is:
    a mistake only in the name, mark your answer A;
    a mistake only in the dollar amount, mark your answer B;
    a mistake in both the name and the dollar amount, mark your answer C;
    no mistake in either the name or the dollar amount, mark your answer D.

SAMPLE QUESTION

Column I
George Peterson
$125.50

Column II
George Petersson
$125.50

Compare the name and dollar amount in Column II with the name and dollar amount in Column I. The name *Petersson* in Column II is spelled *Peterson* in Column I. The amount is the same in both columns. Since there is a mistake only in the name, the answer to the sample question is A. Now answer Questions 1 through 5 in the same manner.

	Column I	Column II	
1.	Susanne Shultz $3440	Susanne Schultz $3440	1.____
2.	Anibal P. Contrucci $2121.61	Anibel P. Contrucci $2112.61	2.____
3.	Eugenio Mendoza $12.45	Eugenio Mendozza $12.45	3.____
4.	Maurice Gluckstadt $4297	Maurice Gluckstadt $4297	4.____
5.	John Pampellonne $4656.94	John Pammpellonne $4566.94	5.____

Questions 6-11.

DIRECTIONS: Each of Questions 6 through 11 consist of a set of names and addresses, which you are to compare. In each question, the name and addresses in Column II should be an EXACT copy of the name and address in Column I. If there is:
- a mistake only in the name, mark your answer A;
- a mistake only in the address, mark your answer B;
- a mistake in both the name and address, mark your answer C;
- no mistake in either the name or address, mark your answer D.

SAMPLE QUESTION

Column I	Column II
Michael Filbert	Michael Filbert
456 Reade Street	645 Reade Street
New York, N.Y. 10013	New York, N.Y. 10013

Since there is a mistake only in the address (the street number should be 456 instead of 645), the answer to the sample question is B. Now answer Questions 6 through 11 in the same manner.

	Column I	Column II	
6.	Hilda Goettelmann 55 Lenox Rd. Brooklyn, N.Y. 11226	Hilda Goetteleman 55 Lenox Ave. Brooklyn, N.Y. 11226	6.____
7.	Arthur Sherman 2522 Batchelder St. Brooklyn, N.Y. 11235	Arthur Sharman 2522 Batcheder St. Brooklyn, N.Y. 11253	7.____
8.	Ralph Barnett 300 West 28 Street New York, New York 10001	Ralph Barnett 300 West 28 Street New York, New York 10001	8.____
9.	George Goodwin 135 Palmer Avenue Staten Island, New York 10302	George Godwin 135 Palmer Avenue Staten Island, New York 10302	9.____
10.	Alonso Ramirez 232 West 79 Street New York, N.Y. 10024	Alonso Ramirez 223 West 79 Street New York, N.Y. 10024	10.____
11.	Cynthia Graham 149-34 83 Street Howard Beach, N.Y. 11414	Cynthia Graham 149-35 83 Street Howard Beach, N.Y. 11414	11.____

3 (#2)

Questions 12-20.

DIRECTIONS: Questions 12 through 20 are problems in subtraction. For each question do the subtraction and select your answer from the four choices given.

12. 232,921.85
     -179,587.68

     A. 52,433.17   B. 52,434.17
     C. 53,334.17   D. 53,343,17

12._____

13. 5,531,876.29
     -3,897,158.36

     A. 1,634,717.93   B. 1,644,718.93
     C. 1,734,717.93   D. 1,7234,718.93

13._____

14. 1,482,658.22
     -937,925.76

     A. 544,633.46   B. 544,732.46
     C. 545,632.46   D. 545,732.46

14._____

15. 937,828.17
     -259,673.88

     A. 678,154.29   B. 679,154.29
     C. 688,155.39   D. 699,155.39

15._____

16. 760,412.38
     -263,465.95

     A. 496,046.43   B. 496,946.43
     C. 496,956.43   D. 497,046.43

16._____

17. 3,203,902.26
     -2,933,087.96

     A. 260,814.30   B. 269,824.30
     C. 270,814.30   D. 270,824.30

17._____

18. 1,023,468.71
     -934,678.88

     A. 88,780.83   B. 88,789.83
     C. 88,880.83   D. 88,889.83

18._____

121

19. 831,549.47
    -772,814.78

    A. 58,734.69   B. 58,834.69
    C. 59,735.69   D. 59,834.69

20. 6,306,181.74
    -3,617,376.99

    A. 2,687,904.99   B. 2,688,904.99
    C. 2,689,804.99   D. 2,799,905.99

Questions 21-30.

DIRECTIONS: Each of Questions 21 through 30 consists of three lines of code letters and three lines of numbers. The numbers on each line should correspond with the code letters on the same line in accordance with the table below.

Code Letter	J	U	B	T	Y	D	K	R	L	P
Corresponding Number	0	1	2	3	4	5	5	7	8	9

On some of the lines, an error exists in the coding. Compare the letters and numbers in each question carefully. If you find an error or errors on:
only *one* of the lines in the question, mark your answer A;
any *two* lines in the question, mark your answer B;
all *three* lines in the question, mark your answer C;
none of the lines in the question, mark your answer D.

SAMPLE QUESTION

BJRPYUR   2079417
DTBPYKJ   5328460
YKLDBLT   4685283

In the above sample, the first line is correct since each code letter listed has the correct corresponding number. On the second line, an error exists because code letter P should have the number 9 instead of the number 8. The third line is correct since each code letter listed has the correct corresponding number. Since there is an error in *one* of the three lines, the correct answer is A. Now answer Questions 21 through 30 in the same manner.

21. BYPDTJL   2495308
    PLRDTJU   9815301
    DTJRYLK   5207486

22. RPBYRJK   7934706
    PKTYLBU   9624821
    KDLPJYR   6489047

5 (#2)

23.	TPYBUJR	3942107	23.____
	BYRKPTU	2476931	
	DUKPYDL	5169458	
24.	KBYDLPL	6345898	24.____
	BLRKBRU	2876261	
	JTULDYB	0318542	
25.	LDPYDKR	8594567	25.____
	BDKDRJL	2565708	
	BDRPLUJ	2679810	
26.	PLRLBPU	9858291	26.____
	LPYKRDJ	88936750	
	TDKPDTR	3569527	
27.	RKURPBY	7617924	27.____
	RYUKPTJ	7426930	
	RTKPTJD	7369305	
28.	DYKPBJT	5469203	28.____
	KLPJBTL	6890238	
	TKPLBJP	3698209	
29.	BTPRJYL	2397148	29.____
	LDKUTYR	8561347	
	YDBLRPJ	4528190	
30.	ULPBKYT	1892643	30.____
	KPDTRBJ	6953720	
	YLKJPTB	4860932	

KEY (CORRECT ANSWERS)

1.	A	11.	D	21.	B
2.	C	12.	C	22.	C
3.	A	13.	A	23.	D
4.	D	14.	B	24.	B
5.	C	15.	A	25.	A
6.	C	16.	B	26.	C
7.	C	17.	C	27.	A
8.	D	18.	B	28.	D
9.	A	19.	A	29.	B
10.	B	20.	B	30.	D

NAME AND NUMBER COMPARISONS

COMMENTARY

This test seeks to measure your ability and disposition to do a job carefully and accurately, your attention to exactness and preciseness of detail, your alertness and versatility in discerning similarities and differences between things, and your power in systematically handling written language symbols.

It is actually a test of your ability to do academic and/or clerical work, using the basic elements of verbal (qualitative) and mathematical (quantitative) learning—words <u>and</u> numbers.

EXAMINATION SECTION

TEST 1

DIRECTIONS: Questions 1 through 6 consist of sets of names and addresses. In each question, the name and address in Column II should be an exact copy of the name and address in Column II. *PRINT IN THE SPACE AT THE RIGHT THE LETTER*
    A. if there is a mistake only in the name
    B. if there is a mistake only in the address
    C. if there is a mistake in both name and address
    D. If there is no mistake in either name or address

SAMPLE:
Michael Filbert
456 Reade Street
New York, N.Y. 10013

Michael Filbert
644 Reade Street
New York, N.Y. 10013

Since there is a mistake only in the address, the answer is B.

1. Esta Wong
   141 West 68 St
   New York, N.Y. 10023

   Esta Wang
   141 West 68 St.
   New York, N.Y. 10023

   1.____

2. Dr. Alberto Grosso
   3475 12th Avenue
   Brooklyn, N.Y. 11218

   Dr. Alberto Grosso
   3475 12th Avenue
   Brooklyn, N.Y. 11218

   2.____

3. Mrs. Ruth Bortlas
   482 Theresa Ct.
   Far Rockaway, N.Y. 11691

   Ms. Ruth Bortias
   482 Theresa Ct.
   Far Rockaway, N.Y. 11169

   3.____

4. Mr. and Mrs. Howard Fox
   2301 Sedgwick Ave.
   Bronx, N.Y. 10468

   Mr. and Mrs. Howard Fox
   231 Sedgwick Ave.
   Bronx, N.Y. 10468

   4.____

5. Miss Marjorie Black
   223 East 23 Street
   New York, N.Y. 10010

   Miss Margorie Black
   223 East 23 Street
   New York, N.Y. 10010

   5.____

2 (#1)

6. Michelle Herman　　　　Michelle Hermann　　　　　　　　　　6._____
   806 Valley Rd.　　　　　806 Valley Dr.
   Old Tappan, N.J. 07675　Old Tappan, N.J. 07675

KEY (CORRECT ANSWERS)

1. A
2. D
3. C
4. B
5. A
6. C

TEST 2

DIRECTIONS: Questions 1 through 6 consist of sets of names and addresses. In each question, the name and address in Column II should be an exact copy of the name and address in Column II. *PRINT IN THE SPACE AT THE RIGHT THE LETTER*

    A. if there is a mistake only in the name
    B. if there is a mistake only in the address
    C. if there is a mistake in both name and address
    D. If there is no mistake in either name or address

1. Ms. Joan Kelly
   313 Franklin Ave.
   Brooklyn, N.Y. 11202

   Ms. Joan Kielly
   318 Franklin Ave.
   Brooklyn, N.Y. 11202

   1.____

2. Mrs. Eileen Engel
   47-24 86 Road
   Queens, N.Y. 11122

   Mrs. Ellen Engel
   47-24 86 Road
   Queens, N.Y. 11122

   2.____

3. Marcia Michaels
   213 E. 81 St.
   New York, N.Y. 10012

   Marcia Michaels
   213 E. 81 St.
   New York, N.Y. 10012

   3.____

4. Rev. Edward J. Smyth
   1401 Brandeis Street
   San Francisco, Calif. 96201

   Rev. Edward J. Smyth
   1401 Brandies Street
   San Francisco, Calif. 96201

   4.____

5. Alicia Rodriguez
   24-68 81 St.
   Elmhurst, N.Y. 11122

   Alicia Rodriquez
   2468 81 St.
   Elmhurst, N.Y. 11122

   5.____

6. Ernest Eissemann
   21 Columbia St.
   New York, N.Y. 10007

   Ernest Eisermann
   21 Columbia St.
   New York, N.Y. 10007

   6.____

KEY (CORRECT ANSWERS)

1. C
2. A
3. D
4. B
5. C
6. A

TEST 3

DIRECTIONS: Questions 1 through 8 consist of names, locations, and telephone numbers. In each question, the name, location and number in Column II should be an exact copy of the name, location, and number in Column I. *PRINT IN THE SPACE AT THE RIGHT THE LETTER*
    A. if there is a mistake in one line only
    B. if there is a mistake in two lines only
    C. if there is a mistake in three lines only
    D. if there are no mistakes in any of the lines

1. Ruth Lang
EAM Bldg., Room C101
625-2000, ext. 765

   Ruth Lang
EAM Bldg., Room C110
625-2000, ext. 765

   1._____

2. Anne Marie Ionozzi
Investigations, Room 827
576-4000, ext. 832

   Anna Marie Ionozzi
Investigation, Room 827
566-4000, ext. 832

   2._____

3. Willard Jameson
Fm C Bldg. Room 687
454-3010

   Willard Jamieson
Fm C Bldg. Room 687
454-3010

   3._____

4. Joanne Zimmermann
Bldg. SW, Room 314
532-4601

   Joanne Zimmermann
Bldg. SW, Room 314
532-4601

   4._____

5. Carlyle Whetstone
Payroll Division-A, Room 212A
262-5000, ext. 471

   Caryle Whetstone
Payroll Division-A, Room 212A
262-5000, ext. 417

   5._____

6. Kenneth Chiang
Legal Council, Room 9745
(201) 416-9100, ext. 17

   Kenneth Chiang
Legal Counsel, Room 9745
(201) 416-9100, ext. 17

   6._____

7. Ethel Koenig
Personnel Services Div, Rm 433
635-7572

   Ethel Hoenig
Personal Services Div, Rm 433
635-7527

   7._____

8. Joyce Ehrhardt
Office of Administrator, Rm W56
387-8706

   Joyce Ehrhart
Office of Administrator, Rm W56
387-7806

   8._____

KEY (CORRECT ANSWERS)

1. A   6. A
2. C   7. C
3. A   8. B
4. D
5. B

TEST 4

DIRECTIONS: Each of Questions 1 through 10 gives the identification number and name of a person who has received treatment at a certain hospital. You are to choose the option (A, B, C, or D) which has EXACTLY the same number and name as those given in the question.

SAMPLE QUESTION:
123765 Frank Y. Jones
- A. 123675 Frank Y. Jones
- B. 123765 Frank T. Jones
- C. 123765 Frank Y. Jones
- D. 123765 Frank Y. Jones

The correct answer is D, because it is the only option showing the identification number and name exactly as they are in the sample question.

1. 754898 Diane Malloy
   - A. 745898 Diane Malloy
   - B. 754898 Dion Malloy
   - C. 754898 Diane Malloy
   - D. 754898 Diane Maloy

2. 661818 Ferdinand Figueroa
   - A. 661818 Ferdinand Figeuroa
   - B. 661618 Ferdinand Figueroa
   - C. 661818 Ferdnand Figueroa
   - D. 661818 Ferdinand Figueroa

3. 100101 Norman D. Braustein
   - A. 100101 Norman D. Braustein
   - B. 101001 Norman D. Braustein
   - C. 100101 Norman P. Braustien
   - D. 100101 Norman D. Bruastein

4. 838696 Robert Kittredge
   - A. 838969 Robert Kittredge
   - B. 838696 Robert Kittredge
   - C. 388696 Robert Kittredge
   - D. 838696 Robert Kittridge

5. 243716 Abraham Soletsky
   - A. 243716 Abrahm Soletsky
   - B. 243716 Abraham Solestky
   - C. 243176 Abraham Soletsky
   - D. 243716 Abraham Soletsky

6. 981121 Phillip M. Maas
   - A. 981121 Phillip M. Mass
   - B. 981211 Phillip M. Maas
   - C. 981121 Phillip M. Maas
   - D. 981121 Phillip N. Maas

7. 786556 George Macalusso
   - A. 785656 George Macalusso
   - B. 786556 George Macalusso
   - C. 786556 George Maculusso
   - D. 786556 George Macluasso

8. 639472 Eugene Weber
   - A. 639472 Eugene Weber
   - B. 639472 Eugene Webre
   - C. 693472 Eugene Weber
   - D. 639742 Eugene Weber

9. 724936 John J. Lomonaco
    A. 724936 John J. Lomanoco
    B. 724396 John L. Lomonaco
    C. 7224936 John J. Lomonaco
    D. 724936 John J. Lamonaco

10. 899868 Michael Schnitzer
    A. 899868 Micheal Schnitzer
    B. 898968 Michael Schnizter
    C. 899688 Michael Schnitzer
    D. 899868 Michael Schnitzer

KEY (CORRECT ANSWERS)

1. C   6. C
2. D   7. B
3. A   8. A
4. B   9. C
5. D   10. D

NAME AND NUMBER CHECKING

EXAMINATION SECTION

TEST 1

DIRECTIONS: Questions 1 through 17 consist of sets of names and addresses. In each question, the name and address in Column II should be an exact copy of the name and address in Column I.
If there is:
a mistake only in the name, mark your answer A;
a mistake only in the address, mark your answer B;
a mistake in both name and address, mark your answer C;
No mistake in either name or address, mark your answer D.

Sample Question

Column I	Column II
Christina Magnusson	Christina Magnusson
288 Greene Street	288 Greene Street
New York, N.Y. 10003	New York, N.Y. 10013

Since there is a mistake only in the address (the zip code should be 10003 instead of 10013), the answer to the sample question is B.

COLUMN I	COLUMN II	
1. Ms. Joan Kelly 313 Franklin Avenue Brooklyn, N.Y. 11202	Ms. Joan Kielly 318 Franklin Ave. Brooklyn, N.Y. 11202	1.____
2. Mrs. Eileen Engel 47-24 86 Road Queens, N.Y. 11122	Mrs. Ellen Engel 47-24 86 Road Queens, New York 11122	2.____
3. Marcia Michaels 213 E. 81 St. New York, N.Y. 10012	Marcia Michaels 213 E. 81 St. New York, N.Y. 10012	3.____
4. Rev. Edward J. Smyth 1401 Brandeis Street San Francisco, Calif. 96201	Rev. Edward J. Smyth 1401 Brandies Street San Francisco, Calif. 96201	4.____
5. Alicia Rodriguez 24-68 82 St. Elmhurst, N.Y. 11122	Alicia Rodriguez 2468 81 St. Elmhurst, N.Y. 11122	5.____

2 (#1)

COLUMN I	COLUMN II	
6. Ernest Eisemann 21 Columbia St. New York, N.Y. 10007	Ernest Eisermann 21 Columbia St. New York, N.Y. 10007	6.____
7. Mr. & Mrs. George Petersson 87-11 91st Avenue Woodhaven, N.Y. 11421	Mr. & Mrs. George Peterson 87-11 91st Avenue Woodhaven, N.Y. 11421	7.____
8. Mr. Ivan Klebnikov 1848 Newkirk Avenue Brooklyn, N.Y. 11226	Mr. Ivan Klebikov 1848 Newkirk Avenue Brooklyn, N.Y. 11622	8.____
9. Mr. Samuel Rothfleisch 71 Pine Street New York, N.Y. 10005	Samuel Rothfleisch 71 Pine Street New York, N.Y. 100005	9.____
10. Mrs. Isabel Tonnessen 198 East 185th Street Bronx, N.Y. 10458	Mrs. Isabel Tonnessen 189 East 185th Street Bronx, N.Y. 10348	10.____
11. Esteban Perez 173 Eighth Street Staten Island, N.Y. 10306	Estaban Perez 173 Eighth Street Staten Island, N.Y. 10306	11.____
12. Esta Wong 141 West 68 St. New York, N.Y. 10023	Esta Wang 141 West 68 St. New York, N.Y. 10023	12.____
13. Dr. Alberto Grosso 3475 12th Avenue Brooklyn, N.Y. 11218	Dr. Alberto Grosso 3475 12th Avenue Brooklyn, N.Y. 11218	13.____
14. Mrs. Ruth Bortias 482 Theresa Ct. Far Rockaway, N.Y. 11691	Ms. Ruth Bortlas 482 Theresa Ct. Far Rockaway, N.Y. 11169	14.____
15. Mr. & Mrs. Howard Fox 2301 Sedgwick Ave. Bronx, N.Y. 10468	Mr. & Mrs. Howard Fox 231 Sedgwick Ave. Bronx, N.Y. 10468	15.____
16. Miss Marjorie Black 223 East 23 Street New York, N.Y. 10010	Miss Margorie Black 223 East 23 Street New York, N.Y. 10010	16.____

3 (#1)

COLUMN I	COLUMN II	
17. Michelle Herman 806 Valley Rd. Old Tappan, N.J. 07675	Michelle Hermann 806 Valley Dr. Old Tappan, N.J. 07675	17.____

KEY (CORRECT ANSWERS)

1.	C	7.	A	13.	D
2.	A	8.	C	14.	C
3.	D	9.	D	15.	B
4.	B	10.	B	16.	A
5.	B	11.	A	17.	C
6.	A	12.	D		

TEST 2

DIRECTIONS: Questions 1 through 15 are to be answered SOLELY on the instructions given below. *PRINT THE LETTER OF THE CORRECT ANSWER IN THE SPACE AT THE RIGHT.*

INSTRUCTIONS

In each of the following questions, the 3-line name and address in Column I is the masterlist entry, and the 3-line entry in Column II is the information to be checked against the master list. If there is one line that does not match, mark your answer A; if there are two lines that do not match, mark your answer B; if all three lines do not match, mark your answer C; if the lines all match exactly, mark your answer D.

Sample Question

Column I
Mark L. Field
11-09 Price Park Blvd.
Bronx, N.Y. 11402

Column II
Mark L. Field
11-99 Prince Park Way
Bronx, N.Y. 11401

The first lines in each column match exactly. The second lines do not match since 11-09 does not match 11-99; and Blvd. does not match Way. The third lines do not match either since 11402 does not match 11401. Therefore, there are two lines that do not match, and the CORRECT answer is B.

	COLUMN I	COLUMN II	
1.	Jerome A. Jackson 1243 14th Avenue New York, N.Y. 10023	Jerome A. Johnson 1234 14th Avenue New York, N.Y. 10023	1.____
2.	Sophie Strachtheim 33-28 Connecticut Ave. Far Rockaway, N.Y. 11697	Sophie Strachtheim 33-28 Connecticut Ave. Far Rockaway, N.Y. 11697	2.____
3.	Elisabeth N.T. Gorrell 256 Exchange St. New York, N.Y. 10013	Elizabeth N.T. Gorrell 256 Exchange St. New York, N.Y. 10013	3.____
4.	Maria J. Gonzalez 7516 E. Sheepshead Rd. Brooklyn, N.Y. 11240	Maria J. Gonzalez 7516 N. Shepshead Rd. Brooklyn, N.Y. 11240	4.____
5.	Leslie B. Brautenweiler 21 57A Seiler Terr. Flushing, N.Y. 11367	Leslie B. Brautenwieler 21-75A Seiler Terr. Flushing, N.J. 11367	5.____

2 (#2)

	COLUMN I	COLUMN II	

6. Rigoberto J. Peredes
157 Twin Towers, #18F
Tottenville, S. I., N.Y,

    Rigoberto J. Peredes
157 Twin Towers, #18F
Tottenville, S.I., N.Y.

    6._____

7. Pietro F. Albino
P.O. Box 7548
Floral Park, N.Y. 11005

    Pietro F. Albina
P.O. Box 7458
Floral Park, N.Y. 11005

    7._____

8. Joanne Zimmerman
Bldg. SW, Room 314
532-4601

    Joanne Zimmermann
Bldg. SW, Room 314
532-4601

    8._____

9. Carlyle Whetstone
Payroll Div. –A, Room 212A
262-5000, ext. 471

    Carlyle Whetstone
Payroll Div. –A, Room 212A
262-5000, ext. 417

    9._____

10. Kenneth Chiang
Legal Council, Room 9745
(201) 416-9100, ext. 17

    Kenneth Chiang
Legal Counsel, Room 9745
(201) 416-9100, Ext. 17

    10._____

11. Ethel Koenig
Personnel Services Division,
Room 433; 635-7572

    Ethel Hoenig
Personal Services Division,
Room 433; 635-7527

    11._____

12. Joyce Ehrhardt
Office of the Administrator,
Room W56; 387-8706

    Joyce Ehrhart
Office of the Administrator,
Room W56; 387-7806

    12._____

13. Ruth Lang
EAM Bldg., Room C101
625-2000, ext. 765

    Ruth Lang
EAM Bldg., Room C110
625-2000, ext. 765

    13._____

14. Anne Marie Ionozzi
Investigations, Room 827
576-4000, ext. 832

    Anna Marie Ionozzi
Investigation, Room 827
566-4000, ext. 832

    14._____

15. Willard Jameson
Fm C Bldg., Room 687
454-3010

    Willard Jamieson
Fm C Bldg., Room 687
454-3010

    15._____

KEY (CORRECT ANSWERS)

1. B
2. D
3. A
4. A
5. C
6. D
7. B
8. D
9. B
10. A
11. C
12. B
13. A
14. C
15. A

TEST 3

DIRECTIONS: Questions 1 through 10 are to be answered on the basis of the following instructions. *PRINT THE LETTER OF THE CORRECT ANSWER IN THE SPACE AT THE RIGHT.*

INSTRUCTIONS

For each such set of names, addresses, and numbers listed in Columns I and II, select your answer from the following options:
The names in Columns I and II are different,
The addresses in Columns I and II are different,
The numbers in Columns I and II are different,
The names, addresses, and numbers in Columns I and II are identical.

	COLUMN I	COLUMN II	
1.	Francis Jones 62 Stately Avenue 96-12446	Francis Jones 62 Stately Avenue 96-21446	1.____
2.	Julio Montez 19 Ponderosa Road 56-73161	Julio Montez 19 Ponderosa Road 56-71361	2.____
3.	Mary Mitchell 2314 Melbourne Drive 68-92172	Mary Mitchell 2314 Melbourne Drive 68-92172	3.____
4.	Harry Patterson 25 Dunne Street 14-33430	Harry Patterson 25 Dunne Street 14-34330	4.____
5.	Patrick Murphy 171 West Hosmer Street 93-81214	Patrick Murphy 171 West Hosmer Street 93-18214	5.____
6.	August Schultz 816 St. Clair Avenue 53-40149	August Schultz 816 St. Claire Avenue 53-40149	6.____
7.	George Taft 72 Runnymede Street 47-04033	George Taft 72 Runnymede Street 47-04023	7.____
8.	Angus Henderson 1418 Madison Street 81-76375	Angus Henderson 1318 Madison Street 81-76375	8.____

2 (#3)

COLUMN I	COLUMN II	
9. Carolyn Mazur 12 Riverview Road 38-99615	Carolyn Mazur 12 Rivervane Road 38-99615	9.____
10. Adele Russell 1725 Lansing Lane 72-91962	Adela Russell 1725 Lansing Lane 72-91962	10.____

KEY (CORRECT ANSWERS)

1. C 6. B
2. C 7. C
3. D 8. D
4. C 9. B
5. C 10. A

TEST 4

DIRECTIONS: Questions 1 through 20 test how good you are at catching mistakes in typing or printing. In each question, the name and address in Column II should be an exact copy of the name and address in Column I. Mark your answer
A. If there is no mistake in either name or address;
B. If there is a mistake in both name and address;
C. If there is a mistake only in the name;
D. If there is a mistake only in the address.
PRINT THE LETTER OF THE CORRECT ANSWER IN THE SPACE AT THE RIGHT.

COLUMN I | COLUMN II

1. Milos Yanocek
33-60 14 Street
Long Island City, N.Y. 11011

   Milos Yanocek
33-60 14 Street
Long Island City, N.Y. 11001

   1.____

2. Alphonse Sabattelo
24 Minnetta Lane
New York, N.Y. 10006

   Alphonse Sabbattelo
24 Minetta Lane
New York, N.Y. 10006

   2.____

3. Helen Steam
5 Metropolitan Oval
Bronx, N.Y. 10462

   Helene Stearn
5 Metropolitan Oval
Bronx, N.Y. 10462

   3.____

4. Jacob Weisman
231 Francis Lewis Boulevard
Forest Hills, N.Y. 11325

   Jacob Weisman
231 Francis Lewis Boulevard
Forest Hills, N.Y. 11325

   4.____

5. Riccardo Fuente
134 West 83 Street
New York, N.Y. 10024

   Riccardo Fuentes
134 West 88 Street
New York, N.Y. 10024

   5.____

6. Dennis Lauber
52 Avenue D
Brooklyn, N.Y. 11216

   Dennis Lauder
52 Avenue D
Brooklyn, N.Y. 11216

   6.____

7. Paul Cutter
195 Galloway Avenue
Staten Island, N.Y. 10356

   Paul Cutter
175 Galloway Avenue
Staten Island, N.Y. 10365

   7.____

8. Sean Donnelly
45-58 41 Avenue
Woodside, N.Y. 11168

   Sean Donnelly
45-58 41 Avenue
Woodside, N.Y. 11168

   8.____

9. Clyde Willot
1483 Rockaway Avenue
Brooklyn, N.Y. 11238

   Clyde Willat
1483 Rockaway Avenue
Brooklyn, N.Y. 11238

   9.____

2 (#4)

COLUMN I	COLUMN II	
10. Michael Stanakis 419 Sheriden Avenue Staten Island, N.Y. 10363	Michael Stanakis 419 Sheraden Avenue Staten Island, N.Y. 10363	10.____
11. Joseph DiSilva 63-84 Saunders Road Rego Park, N.Y. 11431	Joseph Disilva 64-83 Saunders Road Rego Park, N.Y. 11431	11.____
12. Linda Polansky 2224 Fendon Avenue Bronx, N.Y. 20464	Linda Polansky 2255 Fenton Avenue Bronx, N.Y. 10464	12.____
13. Alfred Klein 260 Hillside Terrace Staten Island, N.Y. 15545	Alfred Klein 260 Hillside Terrace Staten Island, N.Y. 15545	13.____
14. William McDonnell 504 E. 55 Street New York, N.Y. 10103	William McConnell 504 E. 55 Street New York, N.Y. 10108	14.____
15. Angela Cipolla 41-11 Parson Avenue Flushing, N.Y. 11446	Angela Cipola 41-11 Parsons Avenue Flushing, N.Y. 11446	15.____
16. Julie Sheridan 1212 Ocean Avenue Brooklyn, N.Y. 11237	Julia Sheridan 1212 Ocean Avenue Brooklyn, N.Y. 11237	16.____
17. Arturo Rodriguez 2156 Cruger Avenue Bronx, N.Y. 10446	Arturo Rodrigues 2156 Cruger Avenue Bronx, N.Y. 10446	17.____
18. Helen McCabe 2044 East 19 Street Brooklyn, N.Y. 11204	Helen McCabe 2040 East 19 Street Brooklyn, N.Y. 11204	18.____
19. Charles Martin 526 West 160 Street New York, N.Y. 10022	Charles Martin 526 West 160 Street New York, N.Y. 10022	19.____
20. Morris Rabinowitz 31 Avenue M Brooklyn, N.Y. 11216	Morris Rabinowitz 31 Avenue N Brooklyn, N.Y. 11216	20.____

KEY (CORRECT ANSWERS)

1.	D	11.	B
2.	B	12.	D
3.	C	13.	A
4.	A	14.	B
5.	B	15.	B
6.	C	16.	C
7.	D	17.	C
8.	A	18.	D
9.	B	19.	A
10.	D	20.	D

TEST 5

DIRECTIONS: In copying the addresses below from Column A to the same line in Column B, an Agent-in-Training made some errors. For Questions 1 through 5, if you find that the agent made an error in
only one line, mark your answer A;
only two lines, mark your answer B;
only three lines, mark your answer C;
all four lines, mark your answer D.

EXAMPLE

COLUMN A	COLUMN B
24 Third Avenue	24 Third Avenue
5 Lincoln Road	5 Lincoln Street
50 Central Park West	6 Central Park West
37-21 Queens Boulevard	21-37 Queens Boulevard

Since errors were made on only three lines, namely the second, third, and fourth, the CORRECT answer is C.
PRINT THE LETTER OF THE CORRECT ANSWER IN THE SPACE AT THE RIGHT.

COLUMN A   COLUMN B

1. 57-22 Springfield Boulevard   75-22 Springfield Boulevard   1.____
    94 Gun Hill Road   94 Gun Hill Avenue
    8 New Dorp Lane   8 New Drop Lane
    36 Bedford Avenue   36 Bedford Avenue

2. 538 Castle Hill Avenue   538 Castle Hill Avenue   2.____
    54-15 Beach Channel Drive   54-15 Beach Channel Drive
    21 Ralph Avenue   21 Ralph Avenue
    162 Madison Avenue   162 Morrison Avenue

3. 49 Thomas Street   49 Thomas Street   3.____
    27-21 Northern Blvd.   21-27 Northern Blvd.
    86 125th Street   86 125th Street
    872 Atlantic Ave.   872 Baltic Ave,

4. 261-17 Horace Harding Expwy.   261-17 Horace Harding Pkwy.   4.____
    191 Fordham Road   191 Fordham Road
    6 Victory Blvd.   6 Victoria Blvd.
    552 Oceanic Ave.   552 Ocean Ave.

5. 90-05 38th Avenue   90-05 36th Avenue   5.____
    19 Central Park West   19 Central Park East
    9281 Avenue X   9281 Avenue X
    22 West Farms Square   22 West Farms Square

KEY (CORRECT ANSWERS)

1. C
2. A
3. B
4. C
5. B

TEST 6

DIRECTIONS: For Questions 1 through 10, choose the letter in Column II next to the number which EXACTLY matches the number in Column I. *PRINT THE LETTER OF THE CORRECT ANSWER IN THE SPACE AT THE RIGHT.*

    COLUMN I   COLUMN II

1. 14235
   - A. 13254
   - B. 12435
   - C. 13245
   - D. 14235

   1.____

2. 70698
   - A. 90768
   - B. 60978
   - C. 70698]
   - D. 70968

   2.____

3. 11698
   - A. 11689
   - B. 11986
   - C. 11968
   - D. 11698

   3.____

4. 50497
   - A. 50947
   - B. 50497
   - C. 50749
   - D. 54097

   4.____

5. 69635
   - A. 60653
   - B. 69630
   - C. 69365
   - D. 69635

   5.____

6. 1201022011
   - A. 1201022011
   - B. 1201020211
   - C. 1202012011
   - D. 1021202011

   6.____

7. 3893981389
   - A. 3893891389
   - B. 3983981389
   - C. 3983891389
   - D. 3893981389

   7.____

8. 4765476589
   - A. 4765476598
   - B. 4765476588
   - C. 4765476589
   - D. 4765746589

   8.____

2 (#6)

9. 8679678938
   - A. 8679687938
   - B. 8679678938
   - C. 8697678938
   - D. 8678678938

   9.____

10. 6834836932
    - A. 6834386932
    - B. 6834836923
    - C. 6843836932
    - D. 6834836932

    10.____

Questions 11-15.

DIRECTIONS: For Questions 11 through 15, determine how many of the symbols in Column Z are exactly the same as the symbol in Column Y.
If none is exactly the same, answer A;
If only one symbol is exactly the same, answer B;
If two symbols are exactly the same, answer C;
If three symbols are exactly the same, answer D.

COLUMN Y	COLUMN Z	
11. A123B1266	A123B1366 A123B1266 A133B1366 A123B1266	11.____
12. CC28D3377	CD22D3377 CC38D3377 CC28C3377 CC28D2277	12.____
13. M21AB201X	M12AB201X M21AB201X M21AB201Y M21BA201X	13.____
14. PA383Y744	AP383Y744 PA338Y744 PA388Y744 PA383Y774	14.____
15. PB2Y8893	PB2Y8893 PB2Y8893 PB3Y8898 PB2Y8893	15.____

KEY (CORRECT ANSWERS)

1.	D	6.	A	11.	C
2.	C	7.	D	12.	A
3.	D	8.	C	13.	B
4.	B	9.	B	14.	A
5.	D	10.	D	15.	D

PAYROLL NOTES & RESOURCES

PAYROLL PRINCIPLES

The maintenance of payroll records, processing of payroll changes, and the preparation of payroll registers, salary checks, and related reports are accomplished by the use of electronic equipment or manual methods. All payrolls covering State employees are computer processed, except where it is determined to be impractical. Payrolls are controlled on a change basis. Except for automated actions, changes to the previous payroll are required to be reported by the agencies on prescribed forms. There are two types of payrolls which are computer processed. The first is the *main* or *regular* payroll. Main payrolls and *special* payrolls are assigned to separate processing schedules, and due dates for submission of payroll forms are established accordingly.

Main payrolls are the normal state payrolls processed on the regular biweekly schedule. It is characteristic of such payrolls that they are in the process of being prepared during the period in which the employee is earning the money. All employees are paid on a main payroll unless specifically assigned to a special payroll. Special payrolls are to be established only on the basis of specific instructions from the Department of Audit and Control. Special payrolls have certain characteristics:

   a. They may be hourly or per diem payrolls where steps to initiate payment are taken by the payroll agency only after work has been completed or substantially performed.
   b. They may be payrolls involving temporary employees.
   c. They may be *one-time* payrolls where the employee is paid at the completion of some specific task.

The following payroll change actions are automated for agency payrolls:

   a. All employees on an annual or biweekly pay basis who receive other than a normal biweekly gross payment in the following pay period. Agencies are not required to submit forms for this change.
   b. All employees paid on an hourly or daily rate or fee basis are reduced to a zero amount after each payment. Unless a PR-75 (a form which would change their status) is submitted in the following period, they are not paid.
   c. All employees reported as being separated from service within the pay period, and who receive payment for part of the pay period, are released from the payroll the following period. A form for removal need not be submitted.
   d. All employees restored to the payroll for the sole purpose of lump sum payment of leave accruals or any type of adjustment are released from the payroll the following period. A form for removal need not be submitted.

Special payrolls may be an exception. Some special payrolls are not normalized; the employee receives the same payment as in the previous period unless a PR-75 is submitted.

The Department of Audit and Control is responsible for the accounting, control, and reporting of deductions for payrolls processed by the Department.

Payroll Forms

The following major forms are used by payroll agencies for reporting the information required in the payroll process.

   a. Payroll and Personnel Transaction Form
   b. Transmittal Form Payroll/Personnel Transactions and Payroll Certification
   c. Payroll Deduction Form
   d. Transmittal for Payroll Deduction Forms
   e. Payroll Header File Change Notice
   f. Report of Check Returned for Refund or Exchange

Basic Payroll Information

The payroll agency code, assigned by Audit and Control, is made up of a two-digit department code and a three-digit division or institution code. The five digits in combination represent the payroll agency code. These identification codes are shown on all papers submitted in relation to the payroll process, including forms requesting the release, refund, or exchange of salary checks. Payroll periods are numbered consecutively within the fiscal year from 1 to 26 (or 27). Payroll period numbers are indicated on the payday calendar, prepared and distributed annually by the Department of Audit and Control.

A line item number is used to identify each position in the payroll agency. All line numbers for computer processed payrolls appear on the payroll register as five-digit numbers. If an employee is to be paid from two or more line items during a payroll period, the employee will appear on the payroll in the most recent item only. The employee's gross salary will represent the total amount paid from both items. If this gross salary is payable from items in different appropriations, an adjustment will be made by the Department of Audit and Control on the computer-prepared Appropriations Charge Sheet, based on the split charge information reported on *Payroll and Personnel Transaction Form* by the agency.

Because of the timing and scheduling requirements involved in the processing of payrolls, certain deadlines or due dates have been established for the submission of the required forms to the Departments of Audit and Control and Civil Service. These due dates must be rigidly adhered to. Any payroll or personnel transaction not accomplished in time for submission by the specified due date must be held in the payroll agency for processing with the payroll data for the next payroll period. Payroll agencies will serve their own best interests by establishing strong internal controls and procedures to assure the complete and timely processing of payroll information. In setting forth the due dates, it is to be understood that DAY 1 is the first day of the payroll period (Thursday), and DAY 14 is the last (Wednesday). Intervening days are numbered in sequence.

Payroll and Personnel Transaction Forms

The purpose of the Form is three-fold:
   a. To advise the Department of Audit and Control of changes to be made affecting payroll preparation in terms of adding, changing, or deleting data, and to provide necessary related information.
   b. To provide the Department of Civil Service with information to be used in certification, re-certification, and record keeping.

c. To provide the payroll agency with a record of the basic data concerning payroll and personnel transactions, and to provide a control for further processing of such transactions.

Payroll and Personnel Transaction Forms are submitted to the Departments of Civil Service and Audit and Control under the Transmittal Form.

These are generally separated into three groups. The general rule of thumb is as follows:

Group I - Appointments, Line Changes, or anything involving a title or status change, three parts go to Civil Service. Civil Service approves or disapproves them and sends 1 part to Audit and Control and 1 part is kept by the agency.

Group II - Separations of any type or changes to employee basic information such as name. 1 part to Audit and Control, 1 part to Civil Service, 3 parts kept by the agency.

Group III - Changes in salary or biweekly pay. 1 part sent to Audit and Control, 4 parts kept by the agency.

When an employee leaves state service after being off the payroll for 2 full biweekly pay periods or 4 weeks, they may receive payment for their accrued vacation and overtime not in excess of 30 days each. The only two times they may be immediately paid this lump sum is if they retire or are laid off.

Inconvenience pay is additional compensation over an employee's basic salary which is authorized for employees who are required to work four or more hours between 6:00 P.M. and 6:00 A.M. in their regular tour of duty. Hours worked between 6:00 P.M. and 6:00 A.M. on an overtime basis are not included when determining eligibility for inconvenience pay.

Location pay is additional compensation granted to an employee whose principal place of employment or official station is located in certain parts of the state.

A reallocation is a change in the grade of an existing title with no change in the title.

A reclassification is a change in an existing title. The new title may retain the same salary grade or be allocated to a lower or higher salary grade.

There is an *Index to Transaction Codes for the Classified Service* that is available to assist payroll offices. For example, listed below are some of the codes and what they represent. It is not necessary to memorize them.

	Group I
PREF	Preferred List Appointment
CERT	Recertification
GLASS	Reclassification
PROB COMP	Successful Completion of Probationary Period

	Group II
RETIRED	Retirement
SICK LV	Sick leave of absence without pay or with half pay
TERM LV	Termination of leave - probationary period completed in another agency
MIL LV	Military leave without pay
	Group III
OT INC SF	Overtime including intermittent inconvenienc and partial shift pay
PRM OT	Premium Overtime
STANDBY	Payment for standby-on-call

Salary and Calculation Data

Many of the questions on this section of the exam have traditionally involved calculating salaries. We have provided information on how this is actually done in state payroll departments. This information should be very helpful to you, if you practice using it. We suggest you make up your own possible test questions as well as doing the practice questions we have provided. (One note of caution: The factors and formulas listed below are the actual, real-life formulas. Often on exams, they will give you other factors and formulas to work with. People who actually work in payroll sometimes lose points because they use the actual factors, instead of those given on the exam. Remember, this is an exam, not real-life, so you should work with what is given to you.

Factors and Formulas for the Calculation of Wages

The following factors and formulas are used to compute wages due annual salaried employees.

ANNUAL   a.   Pay basis code ANN (10-day basis)
Annual salaried employees paid on a biweekly basis over the full calendar year.

    <u>365-Day Year</u>
    Biweekly Rate = .038356 x annual salary
    Work Day Rate = .10 x biweekly rate

    <u>366-Day Year</u>
    Biweekly Rate = .038251 x annual salary
    Work Day Rate = .10 x biweekly rate

    NOTE: An exception: State University professional staff paid on an annual (ANN) basis. For these employees, use the 14-day calendar basis for general increases and discretionary increases effective July first when salary due for the period is paid at two different rates. (See CAL pay basis code for 14 day factors.) You shouldn't need to know this for the exam.

    b.   <u>Pay basis code 8AN</u> (8-day basis)
Annual salaried employees paid for 8 days in a biweekly period (10-hour day).

365-Day Year
Biweekly Rate = .038356 x annual salary
Work Day Rate = .125 x biweekly rate

366-Day Year
Biweekly Rate = .038251 x annual salary
Work Day Rate = .125 x biweekly rate

10 MONTH

Pay basis code 10M (10-day basis)
Annual salaried employees paid on a biweekly basis over a 10 month period.

365-Day Year
Biweekly Rate = .046204 x annual salary
Work Day Rate = .10 x biweekly rate

366-Day Year
Biweekly Rate = .046052 x annual salary
Work Day Rate = .10 x biweekly rate

NOTE: An exception: 10-month employees are paid on the following 14-day calendar basis during the first and the last payroll periods of school year.

365-Day Year and 366-Day Year
Calendar Day Rate = .0714286 x biweekly rate

21 PERIOD or COLLEGE YEAR-PART

Pay basis code 21P or CYP (14-day basis)
Annual salaried employees paid on a biweekly basis over 21 biweekly pay periods.

21 Periods
Biweekly Rate = .047619 x annual salary
Calendar Day Rate = .0714286 x biweekly rate

CALENDAR or COLLEGE YEAR-FULL

Pay basis code CAL or CYF (14-day basis)
Annual salaried employees paid on a biweekly basis over the full calendar year.

365-Day Year
Biweekly Rate = .038356 x annual salary
Calendar Day Rate = .0714286 x biweekly rate

366-Day Year
Biweekly Rate = .038356 x annual salary
Calendar Day Rate = .0714286 x biweekly rate

Calculation of Wages

The following prescribed methods and formulas MUST be used in calculating wages due. In all instances, mills must be dropped after each separate calculation.

ADDITIONAL SALARY FACTORS	When applying additional salary factors such as location pay, inconvenience pay, geographic and shift differentials, premium overtime, and premium holiday, add the annual amount of additional payment to basic annual salary. Multiply the total annual by the biweekly factor to obtain the biweekly rate. If preshift briefing pay is also applicable, add this amount to the biweekly rate.
BIWEEKLY RATE	Total annual salary x biweekly factor = biweekly rate
WORK DAY RATE	Pay basis codes *ANN, *10M, and BIW are processed as having 10 work days in a biweekly period. The work day rate is 1/10 of the biweekly rate.

Biweekly rate x .10 = work day rate

*An exception is made for pay basis codes ANN for State University professional staff and 10M during the first and last payroll periods of the school year. All those times the 14 day calendar rate is used (biweekly rate x .0714286).

Pay basis code 8AN processed as having a 10-hour work day, 4 days per week. The work day rate is 1/8 of the biweekly rate.

Biweekly rate x .125 = work day rate

Pay basis codes 14D, CAL, 21P, CYF, CYP, and SES are processed on a 14-day biweekly basis. The calendar day rate is 1/14 of the biweekly rate.

Biweekly rate x .0714286 = calendar day rate |
| LOST TIME AMOUNT | The amount to be deducted from biweekly wages for lost time is calculated as follows:

Work day rate x number of days lost = lost time amount |
| OVERTIME RATE | Payment for overtime service (hours worked in excess of 40 hours in any work week) is made at one and one-half times the hourly rate of pay for the position in which the overtime is rendered. The overtime compensation rate is determined as follows:

Pay Basis
ANN, 8AN
Annual Salary   x   .00075   = 1 1/2 hourly rate
BIW Biweekly Rate x   .0125   x 1.5   = 1 1/2 hourly rate
DLY Daily Rate   x   .125   x 1.5   = 1 1/2 hourly rate
HRY Hourly Rate   x   1.5   = 1 1/2 hourly rate |

EXTRA SERVICE RATE	A.	Payment due for extra service is determined in the same manner as for overtime, except that a straight hourly rate is paid for any hours required to bring the total work week to the 40-hour basis. The straight time extra service rate is determined as follows:

Pay Basis ANN (Annual Salary) x .0005 = Straight Hourly Rate

B. When the Extra Service Rate is fixed by the Director of the Budget, the payment due is calculated at the hourly rate shown on the Budget Certificate.

HOLIDAY PAY

Holiday compensation is calculated at the rate of one-tenth of the employee's biweekly rate of compensation for each full day of holiday work and includes appropriate additional salary factors (Pre-shift briefing pay is NOT allowed). Holiday compensation for less than a full day is prorated.

For a full day
Biweekly Rate x .10 = Holiday Pay Amount

For a partial day
Work Day Rate x Decimal Equivalent = Holiday Pay Amount

LUMP SUM PAYMENT

Lump sum payment due for accrued credits is calculated as follows:

Work Day Rate x Number of days of accrued credits = Payment due

Number of days for lump sum payment is always reported in full days, for both full-time and part-time employees.

PART-TIME INCUMBENTS of FULL-TIME POSITIONS

For part-time employees in full-time positions, the full annual salary and percentage of time worked are reported. The following formulas are used to calculate biweekly salary:

Full Biweekly Rate = Annual salary x Biweekly factor

Biweekly Payment = Full Biweekly Rate x Percent of Time Worked

INSTITUTION TEACHERS - ADDITIONAL COMPENSATION

Payment for incumbent Institution Teachers required to perform services during July and August is at an hourly rate, determined as follows:

a. For services performed in a teaching title normally paid at a 1-month rate, Hourly Rate = Annual Salary ÷ 1736

b. For services performed in a position normally paid at a 12 month rate, Hourly Rate = Annual Salary ÷ 2000

Services paid may not exceed 40 hours in any one week.

DECIMAL EQUIVALENTS OF PARTS OF AN HOUR	
Hours	
1/4	= .25
1/2	= .50
3/4	= .75
1	= *1
*1 unit is an hour	

Payroll Deductions

All employee salary deductions as well as employee address and retirement system information, except as noted below, are controlled by the payroll agency. Whenever a payroll deduction is initiated, cancelled, or altered, the agency is responsible for submitting the appropriate information to the Department of Audit and Control on the Payroll Deduction Form.

Some deductions are not handled directly by most agencies. These, like garnishees, court orders, State Health Insurance, union dues are handled by Audit and Control, sometimes with assistance from the Department of Civil Service.

Deductions Greater Than Gross Salary

When an employee's gross salary is adjusted to less than normal by submission of a transaction form, any deduction based on a percentage rate (retirement contributions, social security, and withholding tax) is reduced automatically. The employee's net check must be greater than zero, or a check will not be processed. If, after percentage deductions are taken, the employee's gross salary is insufficient to cover all fixed deductions, some or all of these deductions are cancelled automatically in the following order of precedence:

1. Bonds
2. Retirement Loans
3. Federated Funds
4. Credit Union
5. Credit Union
6. Organization Dues
7. Taxable Maintenance
8. Non-taxable Maintenance
9. Automobile & Homeowners Insurance
10. General Insurance
11. TIAA Life
12. State Health Adjustment
13. State Health Insurance
14. Garnishee
15. Court Order
16. Fixed Federal Tax
17. Fixed State Tax
18. Fixed City Tax
19. Fines
20. Social Security Adjustment
21. Social Security Deficiency
22. Retirement Arrears

These deductions are resumed automatically when the employee's gross salary (after percentage deductions) is sufficient to cover them.

If the employee elects to cancel deductions in an order differing from that listed above, a form is prepared, indicating the deductions to be cancelled. When the employee's salary returns to normal, another form restoring and adjusting deductions as necessary is prepared. It is not necessary to adjust deductions for retirement loans or arrears.

www.ingramcontent.com/pod-product-compliance
Lightning Source LLC
Chambersburg PA
CBHW080734230426
43665CB00020B/2734